# Survival Communications in North Dakota

# John E. Parnell, KK4HWX

**13 – ISBN 978- 1478176145**
**10 – ISBN 1478176148**

Cover design by:
Lynda Colón
FREELANCE GRAPHIC DESIGN &
MARKETING COMMUNICATIONS
www.hirelynda.webs.com

## Titles available in this series:

The above titles are available from your favorite online or brick-and-mortar bookstore or directly from the publisher at Tutor Turtle Press LLC, 1027 S. Pendleton St. – Suite B-10, Easley, SC 29642 or on our website: www.TutorTurtlePress.com.

# TABLE OF CONTENTS

## Appendix A – North Dakota Ham Radio Clubs

### ARRL Affiliated Radio Clubs in North Dakota – By City

## Appendix B – FCC Amateur Radio Licenses in North Dakota by City

# Survival Communications in North Dakota

Perhaps you have prepared for WTSHTF or TEOTWAWKI with respect to food, water, self-defense and shelter. But what about communication?

Whenever there is a disaster (hurricane, earthquake, economic collapse, nuclear war, EMF, solar eruption, etc.), the normal means of communication that we're all reliant upon (cell phone, land line phone, the Internet, etc.) will probably be, at best, sporadic and at worst, non-existent.

As this author sees it, short of smoke signals and mirrors, there are three options for communication in "trying times": (1) GMRS or FRS radios; (2) CB radios; and (3) ham or amateur radio. Let's consider each of these options to come up with the most acceptable one.

## GMRS (General Mobile Radio Service) / FRS (Family Radio Service)

GMRS (General Mobile Radio Service) / FRS (Family Radio Service) radios work optimally over short distances where there is minimal interference. Originally designed to be used as pagers, particularly inside a building or other such confined area, these radios are low-cost and convenient to carry. Unfortunately their small size and light weight comes with a trade-off – short range and short battery life. These radios are supposed to be able to communicate for up to 25-30 miles. Right. That's on level terrain, without buildings or trees getting in the way. While battery life technology is constantly improving, you will need spare batteries to keep communicating or someway of recharging the ones in the radio. In this author's opinion, GMRS/FRS radios are not first choice when concerned with medium or long range communication.

## CB (Citizens Band)

CB (Citizens Band) radios operate in a frequency range originally reserved for ham or amateur radio operation. Because of the overwhelming number of people wishing quick, low-cost, regulation-free communication, the FCC (Federal Communication Commission) split off a portion of the frequency spectrum and allowed anyone to purchase a CB radio and start communicating. No test. No license. Just personal/business communication. Today, CB radios are readily available in such outlets as eBay and Craigslist. This author has seen them at yard/garage/tag sales and at flea markets.

CB radios come in a variety of "flavors." Fixed units, sometimes referred to as base units are intended for home use. For the most part, they derive their power from the utility company. In the event of loss of electricity, most base units can also be connected to a 12-volt battery, like that in your car/truck. If you choose to obtain a fixed unit, make sure you know how to connect the unit to the battery – ahead of time. Trying to figure this out when you're under extra stress is not a good situation.

A second type of CB radio is designed to be mobile, that is, installed in your car/truck. It gets its power from the vehicle's battery. You can either attach an antenna permanently to the vehicle or have a removable, magnetic type antenna.

The third type of CB radio is designed for handheld use. They are small and light. Most weigh less than a pound and operate on batteries. Yes, using batteries in a CB poses the same limitations as those by the GMRS/FRS radios, but have the added advantage that most handheld units come with a cigarette lighter adapter. Comes in handy when you are on the move and wish to be able to communicate both from a vehicle and also when you have to abandon it.

While they have a greater range than GMRS/FRS radios, CB radios are, legally, limited to operate on 40 channels, with a power rating of four (4) watts or less. Yes, it is possible to alter CB radios to get around these limitations, but not legally,

**Ham/Amateur Radio**

Ham/Amateur radio is very appealing. With a ham radio, you are not limited to less than 50 miles, but can communicate with anyone in the world (who also has access to a ham radio, of course).

**Standardized Amateur Radio Prepper Communications Plan**

In the event of a nationwide catastrophic disaster, the nationwide network of Amateur Radio licensed preppers will need a set of standardized meeting frequencies to share information and coordinate activities between various prepper groups. This Standardized Amateur Radio Communications Plan establishes a set of frequencies on the 80 meter, 40 meter, 20 meter, and 2 meter Amateur Radio bands for use during these types of catastrophic disasters.

Routine nets will not be held on all of these frequencies, but preppers are encouraged to use them when coordinating with other preppers on a routine basis. Routine nets may be conducted by The American Preparedness Radio Net (TAPRN) on these or other frequencies as they see fit. However, TAPRN will promote the use of these standardized frequencies by all Amateur Radio licensed preppers during times of catastrophic disaster. The promotion of this Standardized Amateur Radio Communications Plan is encouraged by all means within the prepper community, including via Amateur Radio, Twitter, Facebook, and various blogs.

---

**Standardized Frequencies and Modes**

80 Meters – 3.818 MHz LSB (TAPRN Net: Sundays at 9 PM ET)
40 Meters – 7.242 MHz LSB
40 Meters Morse Code / Digital – 7.073 MHz USB (TAPRN: Sundays at 7:30 PM ET on
    CONTESTIA 4/250)
20 Meters – 14.242 MHz USB
2 Meters – 146.420 MHz FM

---

## Nets and Network Etiquette

In times of nationwide catastrophic disaster, the ability of any one prepper to initiate and sustain themselves as a net control may be limited by the availability of power and other resource shortages. However, all licensed preppers are encouraged to maintain a listening watch on these frequencies as often as possible during a catastrophic disaster. Preppers may routinely announce themselves in the following manner:

• This is [Your Callsign Phonetically] in [Your State], maintaining a listening watch on [Standard Frequency] for any preppers on frequency seeking information or looking to provide information. Please call [Your Callsign Phonetically]. Preppers exchanging information that may require follow up should agree upon a designated time to return to the frequency and provide further information. If other stations are utilizing the frequency at the designated time you return, maintain watch and proceed with your communications when those stations are finished. If your communications are urgent and the stations on frequency are not passing information of a critical nature, interrupt with the word "Break" and request use of the frequency.

For More Information

Catastrophe Network: http://www.catastrophenetwork.org or @CatastropheNet on Twitter The American Preparedness Radio Network: http://www.taprn.com or @TAPRN on Twitter

© 2011 Catastrophe Network, Please Distribute Freely

In order to use a ham radio, legally, one must be licensed to do so by the FCC (other countries have analogous governmental bodies to regulate ham radio). To obtain a license is quite easy – take a test and pay your license fee. There are currently three classes of license – Technician, General, and Amateur Extra. With each of these licenses come specific abilities.

Technician class is the beginning level. The exam consists of 35 multiple choice questions randomly drawn from a pool of 395 questions. The question pool is readily available online for free downloading (http://www.ncvec.org/downloads/Revised%20Element%202.Pdf) or in such publications at *Ham Radio License Manual Revised 2nd Edition* (ISBN 978-0-87259-097-7). The current Technician pool of questions is to be used from July 1, 2010 to June 30, 2014. Be sure the question pool you are studying from is current. You will need to score at least 26 correct to pass. (Do not worry, Morse Code is no longer on the test, although many ham operators use it anyway.) You do not need to take a formal class in order to qualify to take the exam. You can learn the material on your own. Most people spend 10-15 hours studying and then successfully take the exam. The cost of taking the exam is under $20. The exam is given in MANY locations throughout the US. Usually the exam is given by area ham clubs. You do not have to belong to the club to take the exam. Check Appendix A for a listing of clubs in North Dakota.

## Topics for the Technician License in Amateur Radio

The Technician license exam covers such topics as basic regulations, operating practices, and electronic theory, with a focus on VHF and UHF applications. Below is the syllabus for the Technician Class.

### Subelement T1 – FCC Rules, descriptions and definitions for the amateur radio service, operator and station license responsibilities

*[6 Exam Questions – 6 Groups]*

T1A – Amateur Radio services; purpose of the amateur service, amateur-satellite service, operator/primary station license grant, where FCC rules are codified, basis and purpose of FCC rules, meanings of basic terms used in FCC rules

T1B – Authorized frequencies; frequency allocations, ITU regions, emission type, restricted sub-bands, spectrum sharing, transmissions near band edges

T1C – Operator classes and station call signs; operator classes, sequential, special event, and vanity call sign systems, international communications, reciprocal operation, station license licensee, places where the amateur service is regulated by the FCC, name and address on ULS, license term, renewal, grace period

T1D – Authorized and prohibited transmissions

T1E – Control operator and control types; control operator required, eligibility, designation of control operator, privileges and duties, control point, local, automatic and remote control, location of control operator

T1F – Station identification and operation standards; special operations for repeaters and auxiliary stations, third party communications, club stations, station security, FCC inspection

### Subelement T2 – Operating Procedures

*[3 Exam Questions – 3 Groups]*

T2A – Station operation; choosing an operating frequency, calling another station, test transmissions, use of minimum power, frequency use, band plans

T2B – VHF/UHF operating practices; SSB phone, FM repeater, simplex, frequency offsets, splits and shifts, CTCSS, DTMF, tone squelch, carrier squelch, phonetics

T2C – Public service; emergency and non-emergency operations, message traffic handling

### Subelement T3 – Radio wave characteristics, radio and electromagnetic properties, propagation modes

*[3 Exam Questions – 3 Groups]*

T3A – Radio wave characteristics; how a radio signal travels; distinctions of HF, VHF and UHF; fading, multipath; wavelength vs. penetration; antenna orientation

T3B – Radio and electromagnetic wave properties; the electromagnetic spectrum, wavelength vs. frequency, velocity of electromagnetic waves

T3C – Propagation modes; line of sight, sporadic E, meteor, aurora scatter, tropospheric ducting, F layer skip, radio horizon

## Subelement T4 - Amateur radio practices and station setup

*[2 Exam Questions – 2 Groups]*

T4A – Station setup; microphone, speaker, headphones, filters, power source, connecting a computer, RF grounding

T4B – Operating controls; tuning, use of filters, squelch, AGC, repeater offset, memory channels

## Subelement T5 – Electrical principles, math for electronics, electronic principles, Ohm's Law

*[4 Exam Questions – 4 Groups]*

T5A – Electrical principles; current and voltage, conductors and insulators, alternating and direct current

T5B – Math for electronics; decibels, electronic units and the metric system

T5C – Electronic principles; capacitance, inductance, current flow in circuits, alternating current, definition of RF, power calculations

T5D – Ohm's Law

## Subelement T6 – Electrical components, semiconductors, circuit diagrams, component functions

*[4 Exam Groups – 4 Questions]*

T6A – Electrical components; fixed and variable resistors, capacitors, and inductors; fuses, switches, batteries

T6B – Semiconductors; basic principles of diodes and transistors

T6C – Circuit diagrams; schematic symbols

T6D – Component functions

## Subelement T7 – Station equipment, common transmitter and receiver problems, antenna measurements and troubleshooting, basic repair and testing

*[4 Exam Questions – 4 Groups]*

T7A – Station radios; receivers, transmitters, transceivers

T7B – Common transmitter and receiver problems; symptoms of overload and overdrive, distortion, interference, over and under modulation, RF feedback, off frequency signals; fading and noise; problems with digital communications interfaces

T7C – Antenna measurements and troubleshooting; measuring SWR, dummy loads, feedline failure modes

T7D – Basic repair and testing; soldering, use of a voltmeter, ammeter, and ohmmeter

## Subelement T8 – Modulation modes, amateur satellite operation, operating activities, non-voice communications

*[4 Exam Questions – 4 Groups]*

T8A – Modulation modes; bandwidth of various signals

T8B – Amateur satellite operation; Doppler shift, basic orbits, operating protocols

T8C – Operating activities; radio direction finding, radio control, contests, special event stations, basic linking over Internet

T8D – Non-voice communications; image data, digital modes, CW, packet, PSK31

## Subelement T9 – Antennas, feedlines

*[2 Exam Groups – 2 Questions]*

T9A – Antennas; vertical and horizontal, concept of gain, common portable and mobile antennas, relationships between antenna length and frequency

T9B – Feedlines; types, losses vs. frequency, SWR concepts, matching, weather protection, connectors

## Subelement T0 – AC power circuits, antenna installation, RF hazards

*[3 Exam Questions – 3 Groups]*

T0A – AC power circuits; hazardous voltages, fuses and circuit breakers, grounding, lightning protection, battery safety, electrical code compliance

T0B – Antenna installation; tower safety, overhead power lines

T0C – RF hazards; radiation exposure, proximity to antennas, recognized safe power levels, exposure to others

Once your name and call sign are available in the FCC database, you have the privilege of operating on all VHF (2 m) and UHF (70 cm) frequencies above 30 megahertz (MHz) and HF frequencies 80, 40, and 15 meter, and on the 10 meter band using Morse code (CW), voice, and digital mode. For a Technician license in North Dakota, your call sign will consist of a two-letter prefix beginning with K or W, the number zero (0), and a three-letter suffix. The single digit number in the call sign is determined according to which area of the US you obtain your first license. Even though you may move to another state, you keep this number in your call sign. This is also true should you upgrade to a higher license and get a new call sign. The numeral portion of your call sign stays the same.

**Call Sign Numbers**

Below is a chart showing the various numbers and the state(s) in which you would obtain the number.

| Call Sign Number | State(s) |
|---|---|
| 0 | CO, IA, KS, MN, MO, NE, ND, SD |
| 1 | CT, ME, MA, NH, RI, VT |
| 2 | NJ, NY |
| 3 | DE, DC, MD, PA |
| 4 | AL, FL, GA, KY, NC, SC, TN, VA |
| 5 | AR, LA, MS, NM, OK, TX |
| 6 | CA |
| 7 | AZ, ID, MT, NV, OR, WA, UT, WY |
| 8 | MI, OH, WV |
| 9 | IL, IN, WI |

Residents of Alaska may have any of the following call sign prefixes assigned to them: AL0-7, KL0-7, NL0-7, or WL0-7. Likewise, residents of Hawaii may have the prefix AH6-7, KH6-7, NH6-7, or WH6-7 assigned.

Once you obtain your Technician license, do not stop there. Go and get your General license.

General is the second of three ham license classes. Like the Technician license, to get a General license, you merely have to take a 35-question multiple choice exam and pay your license fee. Passing is still at least 26 correct answers and the fee is the same (less than $20). Again the question pool is available for free online (http://www.ncvec.org/page.php?id=358). It is also available in such print publications as *The ARRL General Class License Manual 7th Edition* (ISBN 978-0-87259-811-9). The current General pool of questions is to be used from July 1, 2011 to June 30, 2015. Be sure the question pool you are using is current. Being a bit more comprehensive than the Technician license, the General license usually requires 15-20 hours of study to learn the material. Check Appendix A for a listing of clubs in North Dakota where you might take your exam. Once your name and NEW call sign is listed in the FCC database, you're good to go. For a General license in North Dakota, your call sign will consist of a one-letter prefix beginning with K, N or W, the number zero (0), and a three-letter suffix.

### Topics for the General License in Amateur Radio

The General license exam covers regulations, operating practices and electronic theory. Below is the syllabus for the General Class.

| **Subelement G1 – Commission's Rules** |
|---|
| *(5 Exam Questions – 5 Groups)* |
| G1A – General Class control operator frequency privileges; primary and secondary allocations |
| G1B – Antenna structure limitations; good engineering and good amateur practice, beacon operation; restricted operation; retransmitting radio signals |
| G1C – Transmitter power regulations; data emission standards |
| G1D – Volunteer Examiners and Volunteer Examiner Coordinators; temporary identification |
| G1E – Control categories; repeater regulations; harmful interference; third party rules; ITU regions |

| **Subelement G2 – Operating procedures** |
|---|
| *(5 Exam Questions – 5 Groups)* |
| G2A – Phone operating procedures; USB/LSB utilization conventions; procedural signals; breaking into a OSO in progress; VOX operation |
| G2B – Operating courtesy; band plans, emergencies, including drills and emergency communications |

G2C – CW operating procedures and procedural signals; Q signals and common abbreviations; full break in

G2D – Amateur Auxiliary; minimizing interference; HF operations

G2E – Digital operating; procedures, procedural signals and common abbreviations

## Subelement G3 – Radio wave propagation

*(3 Exam Questions – 3 Groups)*

G3A – Sunspots and solar radiation; ionospheric disturbances; propagation forecasting and indices

G3B – Maximum Usable Frequency; Lowest Usable Frequency; propagation

G3C – Ionospheric layers; critical angle and frequency; HF scatter; Near Vertical Incidence Sky waves

## Subelement G4 – Amateur radio practices

*(5 Exam Questions – 5 Groups)*

G4A – Station Operation and setup

G4B – Test and monitoring equipment; two-tone test

G4C – Interference with consumer electronics; grounding; DSP

G4D – Speech processors; S meters; sideband operation near band edges

G4E – HF mobile radio installations; emergency and battery powered operation

## Subelement G5 – Electrical principles

*(3 Exam Questions – 3 Groups)*

G5A – Reactance; inductance; capacitance; impedance; impedance matching

G5B – The Decibel; current and voltage dividers; electrical power calculations; sine wave root-mean-square (RMS) values; PEP calculations

G5C – Resistors; capacitors and inductors in series and parallel; transformers

## Subelement G6 – Circuit components

*(3 Exam Questions – 3 Groups)*

G6A – Resistors; capacitors; inductors

G6B – Rectifiers; solid state diodes and transistors; vacuum tubes; batteries

G6C – Analog and digital integrated circuits (ICs); microprocessors; memory; I/O devices; microwave ICs (MMICs); display devices

## Subelement G7 – Practical circuits

*(3 Exam Questions – 3 Groups)*

G7A – Power supplies; schematic symbols

G7B – Digital circuits; amplifiers and oscillators

G7C – Receivers and transmitters; filters, oscillators

## Subelement G8 – Signals and emissions

*(2 Exam Questions – 2 Groups)*

G8A – Carriers and modulation; AM; FM; single and double sideband; modulation envelope; overmodulation

G8B – Frequency mixing; multiplication; HF data communications; bandwidths of various modes; deviation

## Subelement G9 – Antennas and feed lines

*(4 Exam Questions – 4 Groups)*

G9A – Antenna feed lines; characteristic impedance and attenuation; SWR calculation, measurement and effects; matching networks

G9B – Basic antennas

G9C – Directional antennas

G9D – Specialized antennas

## Subelement G0 – Electrical and RF safety

*(2 Exam Questions – 2 Groups)*

G0A – RF safety principles, rules and guidelines; routine station elevation

G0B – Safety in the ham shack; electrical shock and treatment, safety grounding, fusing, interlocks, wiring, antenna and tower safety

With a General license, you can use all VHF and UHF frequencies and most of the HF frequencies. You would have access to the 160, 30, 17, 12, and 10 meter bands and access to major parts of the 80, 40, 20, and 15 meter bands. Of course, this is in addition to all bands available to Technician license holders.

Amateur Extra is the third of three ham license classes. Like the Technician and General classes, you merely have to pass a test and pay your fee to get your Amateur Extra license. This class of license is more comprehensive than the lower license classes. The exam is longer – 50 questions – and the minimum passing score is higher – 37. However, once you get your Amateur Extra license, all ham frequencies, VHF, UHF and HF are available for your enjoyment. The Extra exam covers regulations, specialized operating practices, advanced electronics theory, and radio equipment design.

Like for the other license classes, the question pool for the Amateur Extra license is available online for downloading (http://www.ncvec.org/downloads/REVISED%202012-2016%20Extra%20Class%20Pool.doc). It is also available in print form in such publications as *The ARRL Extra Class License Manual Revised 9th Edition* (ISBN 978-0-87259-887-4).

### Topics for the Extra License in Amateur Radio

Below is the syllabus for the Amateur Extra Class for July 1, 2012 to June 30, 2016.

## Subelement E1 – Commission's Rules

*[6 Exam Questions – 6 Groups]*

E1A – Operating Standards: frequency privileges; emission standards; automatic message forwarding; frequency sharing; stations aboard ships or aircraft

E1B – Station restrictions and special operations: restrictions on station location; general operating restrictions, spurious emissions, control operator reimbursement; antenna structure restrictions; RACES operations

E1C – Station control: definitions and restrictions pertaining to local, automatic and remote control operation; control operator responsibilities for remote and automatically controlled stations

E1D – Amateur Satellite service: definitions and purpose; license requirements for space stations; available frequencies and bands; telecommand and telemetry operations; restrictions, and special provisions; notification requirements

E1E – Volunteer examiner program: definitions, qualifications, preparation and administration of exams; accreditation; question pools; documentation requirements

E1F – Miscellaneous rules: external RF power amplifiers; national quiet zone; business communications; compensated communications; spread spectrum; auxiliary stations; reciprocal operating privileges; IARP and CEPT licenses; third party communications with foreign countries; special temporary authority

## Subelement E2 – Operating procedures

*[5 Exam Questions – 5 Groups]*

E2A – Amateur radio in space: amateur satellites; orbital mechanics; frequencies and modes; satellite hardware; satellite operations

E2B – Television practices: fast scan television standards and techniques; slow scan television standards and techniques

E2C – Operating methods: contest and DX operating; spread-spectrum transmissions; selecting an operating frequency

E2D – Operating methods: VHF and UHF digital modes; APRS

E2E – Operating methods: operating HF digital modes; error correction

## Subelement E3 – Radio wave propagation

*[3 Exam Questions – 3 Groups]*

E3A – Propagation and technique, Earth-Moon-Earth communications; meteor scatter

E3B – Propagation and technique, trans-equatorial; long path; gray-line; multi-path propagation

E3C – Propagation and technique, Aurora propagation; selective fading; radio-path horizon; take-off angle over flat or sloping terrain; effects of ground on propagation; less common propagation modes

## Subelement E4 – Amateur practices

*[5 Exam Questions – 5 Groups]*

E4A – Test equipment: analog and digital instruments; spectrum and network analyzers, antenna analyzers; oscilloscopes; testing transistors; RF measurements

E4B – Measurement technique and limitations: instrument accuracy and performance limitations; probes; techniques to minimize errors; measurement of "Q"; instrument calibration

E4C – Receiver performance characteristics, phase noise, capture effect, noise floor, image rejection, MDS, signal-to-noise-ratio; selectivity

E4D – Receiver performance characteristics, blocking dynamic range, intermodulation and cross-modulation interference; 3rd order intercept; desensitization; preselection

E4E – Noise suppression: system noise; electrical appliance noise; line noise; locating noise sources; DSP noise reduction; noise blankers

## Subelement E5 – Electrical principles

*[4 Exam Questions – 4 Groups]*

E5A – Resonance and Q: characteristics of resonant circuits: series and parallel resonance; Q; half-power bandwidth; phase relationships in reactive circuits

E5B – Time constants and phase relationships: RLC time constants: definition; time constants in RL and RC circuits; phase angle between voltage and current; phase angles of series and parallel circuits

E5C – Impedance plots and coordinate systems: plotting impedances in polar coordinates; rectangular coordinates

E5D – AC and RF energy in real circuits: skin effect; electrostatic and electromagnetic fields; reactive power; power factor; coordinate systems

## Subelement E6 – Circuit components

*[6 Exam Questions – 6 Groups]*

E6A – Semiconductor materials and devices: semiconductor materials germanium, silicon, P-type, N-type; transistor types: NPN, PNP, junction, field-effect transistors: enhancement mode; depletion mode; MOS; CMOS; N-channel; P-channel

E6B – Semiconductor diodes

E6C – Integrated circuits: TTL digital integrated circuits; CMOS digital integrated circuits; gates

E6D – Optical devices and toroids: cathode-ray tube devices; charge-coupled devices (CCDs); liquid crystal displays (LCDs); toroids: permeability, core material, selecting, winding

E6E – Piezoelectric crystals and MMICs: quartz crystals; crystal oscillators and filters; monolithic amplifiers

E6F – Optical components and power systems: photoconductive principles and effects, photovoltaic systems, optical couplers, optical sensors, and optoisolators

## Subelement E7 – Practical circuits

*[8 Exam Questions – 8 Groups]*

E7A – Digital circuits: digital circuit principles and logic circuits: classes of logic elements; positive and negative logic; frequency dividers; truth tables

E7B – Amplifiers: Class of operation; vacuum tube and solid-state circuits; distortion and intermodulation; spurious and parasitic suppression; microwave amplifiers

E7C – Filters and matching networks: filters and impedance matching networks: types of networks; types of filters; filter applications; filter characteristics; impedance matching; DSP filtering

E7D – Power supplies and voltage regulators

E7E – Modulation and demodulation: reactance, phase and balanced modulators; detectors; mixer stages; DSP modulation and demodulation; software defined radio systems

E7F – Frequency markers and counters: frequency divider circuits; frequency marker generators; frequency counters

E7G – Active filters and op-amps: active audio filters; characteristics; basic circuit design; operational amplifiers

E7H – Oscillators and signal sources: types of oscillators; synthesizers and phase-locked loops; direct digital synthesizers

## Subelement E8 – Signals and emissions

*[4 Exam Questions – 4 Groups]*

E8A – AC waveforms: sine, square, sawtooth and irregular waveforms; AC measurements; average and PEP of RF signals; pulse and digital signal waveforms

E8B – Modulation and demodulation: modulation methods; modulation index and deviation ratio; pulse modulation; frequency and time division multiplexing

E8C – Digital signals: digital communications modes; CW; information rate vs. bandwidth; spread-spectrum communications; modulation methods

E8D – Waves, measurements, and RF grounding: peak-to-peak values, polarization; RF grounding

## Subelement E9 – Antennas and transmission lines

*[8 Exam Questions – 8 Groups]*

E9A – Isotropic and gain antennas: definition; used as a standard for comparison; radiation pattern; basic antenna parameters: radiation resistance and reactance, gain, beamwidth, efficiency

E9B – Antenna patterns: E and H plane patterns; gain as a function of pattern; antenna design; Yagi antennas

E9C – Wire and phased vertical antennas: beverage antennas; terminated and resonant rhombic antennas; elevation above real ground; ground effects as related to polarization; take-off angles

E9D – Directional antennas: gain; satellite antennas; antenna beamwidth; losses; SWR bandwidth; antenna efficiency; shortened and mobile antennas; grounding

E9E – Matching: matching antennas to feed lines; power dividers

E9F – Transmission lines: characteristics of open and shorted feed lines: 1/8 wavelength; 1/4 wavelength; 1/2 wavelength; feed lines: coax versus open-wire; velocity factor; electrical length; transformation characteristics of line terminated in impedance not equal to characteristic impedance

E9G – The Smith chart

E9H – Effective radiated power; system gains and losses; radio direction finding antennas

*[1 exam question – 1 group]*
E0A – Safety: amateur radio safety practices; RF radiation hazards; hazardous materials

Once your new call sign is listed in the FCC database, you are good to go. For an Amateur Extra license in North Dakota, your call sign will consist of a prefix of K, N or W, the number zero (0), and a two-letter suffix, or a two-letter prefix beginning with A, N, K or W, the number zero (0), and a one-letter suffix, or a two-letter prefix beginning with A, the number zero (0), and a two-letter suffix.

Ham radio equipment can be expensive or you can do it "on the cheap." The cost will run from a couple hundred dollars to well in the thousands, depending on what you have available. eBay, and Craigslist are good places to start looking. Most ham clubs do some sort of hamfest annually wherein club members or others are willing to part with older equipment. See Appendix A for a list of clubs in North Dakota.

Another excellent source of equipment, as well as advice on setting the equipment up and how to use it properly, is current ham operators. In Appendix B, the author has listed all the FCC licensed ham operators in North Dakota, listed by city, and then sorted by street and house number on the street. Who knows, maybe someone who lives close to you is a ham operator. Be a good neighbor, stop by and have a chat with him/her.

Like CB radios, ham radios come in three formats – base, mobile, and handheld. They can use the electric company for power, or operate off a car battery. In the opinion of this author, in spite of the slightly higher cost of the equipment and having to take a test to legally use the equipment, ham radio is the way to go when concerned about communication during times of crisis.

**Canadian Call Sign Prefixes**

Because of our proximity to Canada, many times ham contact is made with our northern neighbors. Below is a chart showing the origin of Canadian call sign prefixes.

| Call Sign Prefix | Provence or Territory |
|---|---|
| CY0 | Sable Island |
| CY9 | St. Paul Island |
| VA1, VE1 | New Brunswick, Nova Scotia |
| VA2, VE2 | Quebec |
| VA3, VE3 | Ontario |
| VA4, VE4 | Manitoba |
| VA5, VE5 | Saskatchewan |
| VA6, VE6 | Alberta |
| VA7, VE7 | British Columbia |
| VE8 | North West Territories |
| VE9 | New Brunswick |
| VO1 | Newfoundland |

| | | |
|---|---|---|
| VO2 | Labrador | |
| VY0 | Nunavut | |
| VY1 | Yukon | |
| VY2 | Prince Edward Island | |

## Common Radio Bands in the United States

Certain radio bands are more popular with ham radio enthusiasts than others. Below is a chart showing these bands and when they are most popular.

| | Band (meter) | Frequency (MHz) | Use |
|---|---|---|---|
| **HF** | 160 | 1.8 – 2.0 | Night |
| | 80 | 3.5 – 4.0 | Night and Local Day |
| | 40 | 7.0 – 7.3 | Night and Local Day |
| | 30 | 10.1 – 10.15 | CW and Digital |
| | 20 | 14.0 – 14.350 | World Wide Day and Night |
| | 17 | 18.068 – 18.168 | World Wide Day and Night |
| | 15 | 21.0 – 21.450 | Primarily Daytime |
| | 12 | 24.890 – 24.990 | Primarily Daytime |
| | 10 | 28.0 – 29.70 | Daytime during Sunspot highs |
| **VHF** | 6 | 50 – 54 | Local to World Wide |
| | 2 | 144 – 148 | Local to Medium Distance |
| **UHF** | 70 cm | 430 – 440 | Local |

## Common Amateur Radio Bands in Canada

### 160 Meter Band - Maximum bandwidth 6 kHz
1.800 - 1.820 MHz - CW
1.820 - 1.830 MHz - Digital Modes
1 830 - 1.840 MHz - DX Window
1.840 - 2.000 MHz - SSB and other wide band modes

### 80 Meter Band - Maximum bandwidth 6 kHz
3.500 - 3.580 MHz - CW
3.580 - 3.620 MHz - Digital Modes
3.620 - 3.635 MHz - Packet/Digital Secondary
3.635 - 3.725 MHz - CW
3.725 - 3.790 MHz - SSB and other side band modes*
3.790 - 3.800 MHz - SSB DX Window
3.800 - 4.000 MHz - SSB and other wide band modes

### 40 Meter Band - Maximum bandwidth 6 kHz
7.000 - 7.035 MHz - CW
7.035 - 7.050 MHz - Digital Modes
7.040 - 7.050 MHz - International packet

7.050 - 7.100 MHz - SSB
7.100 - 7.120 MHz - Packet within Region 2
7.120 - 7.150 MHz - CW
7.150 - 7.300 MHz - SSB and other wide band modes

## 30 Meter Band - Maximum bandwidth 1 kHz

10.100 - 10.130 MHz - CW only
10.130 - 10.140 MHz - Digital Modes
10.140 - 10.150 MHz - Packet

## 20 Meter Band - Maximum bandwidth 6 kHz

14.000 - 14.070 MHz - CW only
14.070 - 14.095 MHz - Digital Mode
14.095 - 14.099 MHz - Packet
14.100 MHz - Beacons
14.101 - 14.112 MHz - CW, SSB, packet shared
14.112 - 14.350 MHz - SSB
14.225 - 14.235 MHz - SSTV

## 17 Meter Band - Maximum bandwidth 6 kHz

18.068 - 18.100 MHz - CW
18.100 - 18.105 MHz - Digital Modes
18.105 - 18.110 MHz - Packet
18.110 - 18.168 MHz - SSB and other wide band modes

## 15 Meter Band - maximum bandwidth 6 kHz

21.000 - 21.070 MHz - CW
21.070 - 21.090 MHz - Digital Modes
21.090 - 21.125 MHz - Packet
21.100 - 21.150 MHz - CW and SSB
21.150 - 21.335 MHz - SSB and other wide band modes
21.335 - 21.345 MHz - SSTV
21.345 - 21.450 MHz - SSB and other wide band modes

## 12 Meter Band - Maximum bandwidth 6 kHz

24.890 - 24.930 MHz - CW
24.920 - 24.925 MHz - Digital Modes
24.925 - 24.930 MHz - Packet
24.930 - 24.990 MHz - SSB and other wide band modes

## 10 Meter Band - Maximum band width 20 kHz

28.000 - 28.200 MHz - CW
28.070 - 28.120 MHz - Digital Modes
28.120 - 28.190 MHz - Packet

28.190 - 28.200 MHz - Beacons
28.200 - 29.300 MHz - SSB and other wide band modes
29.300 - 29.510 MHz - Satellite
29.510 - 29.700 MHz - SSB, FM and repeaters

## 160 Meters (1.8-2.0 MHz)

1.800 - 2.000 CW
1.800 - 1.810 Digital Modes
1.810 CW QRP
1.843-2.000 SSB, SSTV and other wideband modes
1.910 SSB QRP
1.995 - 2.000 Experimental
1.999 - 2.000 Beacons

## 80 Meters (3.5-4.0 MHz)

3.590 RTTY/Data DX
3.570-3.600 RTTY/Data
3.790-3.800 DX window
3.845 SSTV
3.885 AM calling frequency

## 40 Meters (7.0-7.3 MHz)

7.040 RTTY/Data DX
7.080-7.125 RTTY/Data
7.171 SSTV
7.290 AM calling frequency

## 30 Meters (10.1-10.15 MHz)

10.130-10.140 RTTY
10.140-10.150 Packet

## 20 Meters (14.0-14.35 MHz)

14.070-14.095 RTTY
14.095-14.0995 Packet
14.100 NCDXF Beacons
14.1005-14.112 Packet
14.230 SSTV
14.286 AM calling frequency

## 17 Meters (18.068-18.168 MHz)

18.100-18.105 RTTY
18.105-18.110 Packet

## 15 Meters (21.0-21.45 MHz)

21.070-21.110 RTTY/Data

21.340 SSTV

## 12 Meters (24.89-24.99 MHz)

24.920-24.925 RTTY
24.925-24.930 Packet

## 10 Meters (28-29.7 MHz)

28.000-28.070 CW
28.070-28.150 RTTY
28.150-28.190 CW
28.200-28.300 Beacons
28.300-29.300 Phone
28.680 SSTV
29.000-29.200 AM
29.300-29.510 Satellite Downlinks
29.520-29.590 Repeater Inputs
29.600 FM Simplex
29.610-29.700 Repeater Outputs

## 6 Meters (50-54 MHz)

50.0-50.1 CW, beacons
50.060-50.080 beacon subband
50.1-50.3 SSB, CW
50.10-50.125 DX window
50.125 SSB calling
50.3-50.6 All modes
50.6-50.8 Nonvoice communications
50.62 Digital (packet) calling
50.8-51.0 Radio remote control (20-kHz channels)
51.0-51.1 Pacific DX window
51.12-51.48 Repeater inputs (19 channels)
51.12-51.18 Digital repeater inputs
51.5-51.6 Simplex (seven channels)
51.62-51.98 Repeater outputs (19 channels)
51.62-51.68 Digital repeater outputs
52.0-52.48 Repeater inputs (except as noted; 23 channels)
52.02, 52.04 FM simplex
52.2 TEST PAIR (input)
52.5-52.98 Repeater output (except as noted; 23 channels)
52.525 Primary FM simplex
52.54 Secondary FM simplex
52.7 TEST PAIR (output)
53.0-53.48 Repeater inputs (except as noted; 19 channels)
53.0 Remote base FM simplex
53.02 Simplex
53.1, 53.2, 53.3, 53.4 Radio remote control

53.5-53.98 Repeater outputs (except as noted; 19 channels)
53.5, 53.6, 53.7, 53.8 Radio remote control
53.52, 53.9 Simplex

## 2 Meters (144-148 MHz)

144.00-144.05 EME (CW)
144.05-144.10 General CW and weak signals
144.10-144.20 EME and weak-signal SSB
144.200 National calling frequency
144.200-144.275 General SSB operation
144.275-144.300 Propagation beacons
144.30-144.50 New OSCAR subband
144.50-144.60 Linear translator inputs
144.60-144.90 FM repeater inputs
144.90-145.10 Weak signal and FM simplex (145.01,03,05,07,09 are widely used for packet)
145.10-145.20 Linear translator outputs
145.20-145.50 FM repeater outputs
145.50-145.80 Miscellaneous and experimental modes
145.80-146.00 OSCAR subband
146.01-146.37 Repeater inputs
146.40-146.58 Simplex
146.52 National Simplex Calling Frequency
146.61-146.97 Repeater outputs
147.00-147.39 Repeater outputs
147.42-147.57 Simplex
147.60-147.99 Repeater inputs

## 1.25 Meters (222-225 MHz)

222.0-222.150 Weak-signal modes
222.0-222.025 EME
222.05-222.06 Propagation beacons
222.1 SSB & CW calling frequency
222.10-222.15 Weak-signal CW & SSB
222.15-222.25 Local coordinator's option; weak signal, ACSB, repeater inputs, control
222.25-223.38 FM repeater inputs only
223.40-223.52 FM simplex
223.52-223.64 Digital, packet
223.64-223.70 Links, control
223.71-223.85 Local coordinator's option; FM simplex, packet, repeater outputs
223.85-224.98 Repeater outputs only

## 70 Centimeters (420-450 MHz)

420.00-426.00 ATV repeater or simplex with 421.25 MHz video carrier control links and experimental

426.00-432.00 ATV simplex with 427.250-MHz video carrier frequency
432.00-432.07 EME (Earth-Moon-Earth)
432.07-432.10 Weak-signal CW
432.10 70-cm calling frequency
432.10-432.30 Mixed-mode and weak-signal work
432.30-432.40 Propagation beacons
432.40-433.00 Mixed-mode and weak-signal work
433.00-435.00 Auxiliary/repeater links
435.00-438.00 Satellite only (internationally)
438.00-444.00 ATV repeater input with 439.250-MHz video carrier frequency and repeater links
442.00-445.00 Repeater inputs and outputs (local option)
445.00-447.00 Shared by auxiliary and control links, repeaters and simplex (local option)
446.00 National simplex frequency
447.00-450.00 Repeater inputs and outputs (local option)

## 33 Centimeters (902-928 MHz)
902.0-903.0 Narrow-bandwidth, weak-signal communications
902.0-902.8 SSTV, FAX, ACSSB, experimental
902.1 Weak-signal calling frequency
902.8-903.0 Reserved for EME, CW expansion
903.1 Alternate calling frequency
903.0-906.0 Digital communications
906-909 FM repeater inputs
909-915 ATV
915-918 Digital communications
918-921 FM repeater outputs
921-927 ATV
927-928 FM simplex and links

## 23 Centimeters (1240-1300 MHz)
1240-1246 ATV #1
1246-1248 Narrow-bandwidth FM point-to-point links and digital, duplex with 1258-
   1260.
1248-1258 Digital Communications
1252-1258 ATV #2
1258-1260 Narrow-bandwidth FM point-to-point links digital, duplexed with 1246-1252
1260-1270 Satellite uplinks, reference WARC '79
1260-1270 Wide-bandwidth experimental, simplex ATV
1270-1276 Repeater inputs, FM and linear, paired with 1282-1288, 239 pairs every 25
   kHz, e.g. 1270.025, .050, etc.
1271-1283 Non-coordinated test pair
1276-1282 ATV #3
1282-1288 Repeater outputs, paired with 1270-1276
1288-1294 Wide-bandwidth experimental, simplex ATV
1294-1295 Narrow-bandwidth FM simplex services, 25-kHz channels

1294.5 National FM simplex calling frequency
1295-1297 Narrow bandwidth weak-signal communications (no FM)
1295.0-1295.8 SSTV, FAX, ACSSB, experimental
1295.8-1296.0 Reserved for EME, CW expansion
1296.00-1296.05 EME-exclusive
1296.07-1296.08 CW beacons
1296.1 CW, SSB calling frequency
1296.4-1296.6 Crossband linear translator input
1296.6-1296.8 Crossband linear translator output
1296.8-1297.0 Experimental beacons (exclusive)
1297-1300 Digital Communications

## 2300-2310 and 2390-2450 MHz

2300.0-2303.0 High-rate data
2303.0-2303.5 Packet
2303.5-2303.8 TTY packet
2303.9-2303.9 Packet, TTY, CW, EME
2303.9-2304.1 CW, EME
2304.1 Calling frequency
2304.1-2304.2 CW, EME, SSB
2304.2-2304.3 SSB, SSTV, FAX, Packet AM, Amtor
2304.30-2304.32 Propagation beacon network
2304.32-2304.40 General propagation beacons
2304.4-2304.5 SSB, SSTV, ACSSB, FAX, Packet AM, Amtor experimental
2304.5-2304.7 Crossband linear translator input
2304.7-2304.9 Crossband linear translator output
2304.9-2305.0 Experimental beacons
2305.0-2305.2 FM simplex (25 kHz spacing)
2305.20 FM simplex calling frequency
2305.2-2306.0 FM simplex (25 kHz spacing)
2306.0-2309.0 FM Repeaters (25 kHz) input
2309.0-2310.0 Control and auxiliary links
2390.0-2396.0 Fast-scan TV
2396.0-2399.0 High-rate data
2399.0-2399.5 Packet
2399.5-2400.0 Control and auxiliary links
2400.0-2403.0 Satellite
2403.0-2408.0 Satellite high-rate data
2408.0-2410.0 Satellite
2410.0-2413.0 FM repeaters (25 kHz) output
2413.0-2418.0 High-rate data
2418.0-2430.0 Fast-scan TV
2430.0-2433.0 Satellite
2433.0-2438.0 Satellite high-rate data
2438.0-2450.0 WB FM, FSTV, FMTV, SS experimental

| 3300-3500 MHz |
| --- |
| 3456.3-3456.4 Propagation beacons |

| 5650-5925 MHz |
| --- |
| 5760.3-5760.4 Propagation beacons |

| 10.00-10.50 GHz |
| --- |
| 10.368 Narrow band calling frequency 10.3683-10.3684 Propagation beacons |
| 10.3640 Calling frequency |

Now that you have your license (you do, don't you?), and your equipment, you are ready to go live. Below is a suggested start.

1) Assuming you have the HT set up to the appropriate frequency, and offset, press the mic button on the HT and say, "KK4HWX listening." Replace the KK4HWX with your own call sign, the one assigned to you by the FCC (it's the law). If no one responds to your call, you may wish to try again. Hopefully someone will respond to your call.

2) Once you get a response, it will be in the form of something like, "KK4HWX this is ??1??? in Eastport returning. My name is Florence. Back to you. ??1???" then a tone. Let us examine the response more closely. She first acknowledged your call sign (KK4HWX), then identified hers (??1???). From the 1 in her call sign, you know that she first got her license in Region 1, meaning she got it while a resident of CT, ME, MA, NH, RI, or VT. She then told you where she's transmitting from (Eastport). The term "returning" means that she is returning your call. Her name is Florence. The phrase, "Back to you" indicates that she is turning over the conversation to you. She then repeats her call sign. The tone indicates to you that it is okay to proceed with your response. BTW if she had used the term "Over" instead of "Back to you," it would mean the same thing, just fewer words.

3) At this point, press the mic button and continue with the conversation. You should restate your call sign often during the conversation (perhaps every 10 minutes or less and whenever you begin transmitting). Don't forget to say, "Over" or "Back to you" whenever you are giving Florence control of the conversation again.

4) When you are ready to stop the conversation, you should say goodbye or use the phrase "73", meaning "best wishes." Your conversation would end something like, "??1??? 73, this is KK4HWX clear and monitoring." The "clear and monitoring" indicates that you are going to continue to monitor the frequency. If you are not going to continue monitoring, you may wish to end the conversation with Florence with, "clear and QRT" instead. The QRT means that you are stopping transmissions.

**Call Sign Phonics**

Because of different accents of various people, sometimes it is difficult to understand call sign letters when spoken. For this reason, most ham operators verbalize their call sign using phonics. Below is a table listing the accepted phonics for letters and numbers.

A = ALFA
B = BRAVO
C = CHARLIE
D = DELTA
E = ECHO
F = FOXTROT
G = GOLF
H = HOTEL
I = INDIA
J = JULIETT
K = KILO
L = LIMA
M = MIKE
N = NOVEMBER
O = OSCAR
P = PAPA (PA-PA')
Q = QUEBEC (KAY-BEK')
R = ROMEO

S = SIERRA
T = TANGO
U = UNIFORM
V = VICTOR
W = WHISKEY
X = X-RAY
Y = YANKEE
Z = ZULU (ZED)
1 = ONE
2 = TWO
3 = THREE (TREE)
4 = FOUR
5 = FIVE (FIFE)
6 = SEVEN
7 = SEVEN
8 = EIGHT
9 = NINE (NINER)
0 = ZERO

The words in parentheses are the pronunciation or the alternate pronunciations for the words or numbers, but you will hear both used. With the letter Z, (ZED) is by far the most commonly used. With the number 9, NINER is the most common and easiest to understand ON THE AIR.

If you wish to use Morse code (CW) instead of voice communication, the "conversation" would follow the same steps, with a few modifications. To type out each word would require a lot of typing and translating. If you are like this author, more means more, i.e., more typing means more typos are likely. To help with this situation, CW enthusiasts have developed a language all their own – they use abbreviations for common phrases. Below is a chart showing some of these abbreviations.

| Abbreviation | Use |
|--------------|-----|
| AR | Over |
| de | From or "this is" |
| ES | And |
| GM | Good Morning |
| K | Go |
| KN | Go only |
| NM | Name |
| QTH | Location |
| RPT | Report |
| R | Roger |
| SK | Clear |

| tnx | Thanks |
|-----|--------|
| UR | Your, you are |
| 73 | Best Wishes |

## Morse Code and Amateur Radio

If you wish to use CW, but are concerned about accuracy, you might consider purchasing a Morse code translator. This is an electronic device that you place in front of your speakers. It takes the CW sounds and translates them into English and displays the transmission on an LCD display. For the reverse, you can pick up a CW keyboard. With the keyboard, you type in your message and it converts the text to Morse code. The translator does not need to be attached to your ham equipment, whereas the keyboard would.

For your convenience, below is a table showing the Morse code signals and their meaning.

| Character | Code |
|-----------|------|
| A | · — |
| B | — · · · |
| C | — · — · |
| D | — · · |
| E | · |
| F | · · — · |
| G | — — · |
| H | · · · · |
| I | · · |
| J | · — — — |
| K | — · — |
| L | · — · · |
| M | — — |
| N | — · |
| O | — — — |
| P | · — — · |
| Q | — — · — |
| R | · — · |
| S | · · · |
| T | — |
| U | · · — |
| V | · · · — |
| W | · — — |
| X | — · · — |
| Y | — · — — |
| Z | — — · · |
| 0 | — — — — — |
| 1 | · — — — — |

| | |
|---|---|
| 2 | ·· — — — |
| 3 | ··· — — |
| 4 | ···· — |
| 5 | ····· |
| 6 | — ···· |
| 7 | — — ··· |
| 8 | — — — ·· |
| 9 | — — — — · |
| Ampersand [&], Wait | · — ··· |
| Apostrophe ['] | · — — — — · |
| At sign [@] | · — — · — · |
| Colon [:] | — — — ··· |
| Comma [,] | — — ·· — — |
| Dollar sign [$] | ··· — ·· — |
| Double dash [=] | — ··· — |
| Exclamation mark [!] | — · — · — — |
| Hyphen, Minus [-] | — ···· — |
| Parenthesis closed [)] | — · — — · — |
| Parenthesis open [(] | — · — — · |
| Period [.] | · — · — · — |
| Plus [+] | · — · — · |
| Question mark [?] | ·· — — ·· |
| Quotation mark ["] | · — ·· — · |
| Semicolon [;] | — · — · — · |
| Slash [/], Fraction bar | — ·· — · |
| Underscore [_] | ·· — — · — |

An advantage of using Morse Code is that when broadcasting CW, you are using reduced power, thereby saving your battery. Your battery is used only while actually transmitting or receiving.

**International Call Sign Prefixes**

As was stated earlier, all ham radio call signs begin with letters (or numbers) taken from blocks assigned to each country of the world by the *ITU - International Telecommunications Union,* a body controlled by the United Nations. The following chart indicates which call sign series are allocated to which countries.

| Call Sign Series | Allocated to |
|---|---|
| **AAA-ALZ** | **United States of America** |
| AMA-AOZ | Spain |
| APA-ASZ | Pakistan (Islamic Republic of) |
| ATA-AWZ | India (Republic of) |
| AXA-AXZ | Australia |
| AYA-AZZ | Argentine Republic |

| | |
|---|---|
| A2A-A2Z | Botswana (Republic of) |
| A3A-A3Z | Tonga (Kingdom of) |
| A4A-A4Z | Oman (Sultanate of) |
| A5A-A5Z | Bhutan (Kingdom of) |
| A6A-A6Z | United Arab Emirates |
| A7A-A7Z | Qatar (State of) |
| A8A-A8Z | Liberia (Republic of) |
| A9A-A9Z | Bahrain (State of) |
| BAA-BZZ | China (People's Republic of) |
| CAA-CEZ | Chile |
| CFA-CKZ | Canada |
| CLA-CMZ | Cuba |
| CNA-CNZ | Morocco (Kingdom of) |
| COA-COZ | Cuba |
| CPA-CPZ | Bolivia (Republic of) |
| CQA-CUZ | Portugal |
| CVA-CXZ | Uruguay (Eastern Republic of) |
| CYA-CZZ | Canada |
| C2A-C2Z | Nauru (Republic of) |
| C3A-C3Z | Andorra (Principality of) |
| C4A-C4Z | Cyprus (Republic of) |
| C5A-C5Z | Gambia (Republic of the) |
| C6A-C6Z | Bahamas (Commonwealth of the) |
| C7A-C7Z | World Meteorological Organization |
| C8A-C9Z | Mozambique (Republic of) |
| DAA-DRZ | Germany (Federal Republic of) |
| DSA-DTZ | Korea (Republic of) |
| DUA-DZZ | Philippines (Republic of the) |
| D2A-D3Z | Angola (Republic of) |
| D4A-D4Z | Cape Verde (Republic of) |
| D5A-D5Z | Liberia (Republic of) |
| D6A-D6Z | Comoros (Islamic Federal Republic of the) |
| D7A-D9Z | Korea (Republic of) |
| EAA-EHZ | Spain |
| EIA-EJZ | Ireland |
| EKA-EKZ | Armenia (Republic of) |
| ELA-ELZ | Liberia (Republic of) |
| EMA-EOZ | Ukraine |
| EPA-EQZ | Iran (Islamic Republic of) |
| ERA-ERZ | Moldova (Republic of) |
| ESA-ESZ | Estonia (Republic of) |
| ETA-ETZ | Ethiopia (Federal Democratic Republic of) |
| EUA-EWZ | Belarus (Republic of) |
| EXA-EXZ | Kyrgyz Republic |
| EYA-EYZ | Tajikistan (Republic of) |

| | |
|---|---|
| EZA-EZZ | Turkmenistan |
| E2A-E2Z | Thailand |
| E3A-E3Z | Eritrea |
| E4A-E4Z | Palestinian Authority |
| E5A-E5Z | New Zealand - Cook Islands (WRC-07) |
| E7A-E7Z | Bosnia and Herzegovina (Republic of) (WRC-07) |
| FAA-FZZ | France |
| GAA-GZZ | United Kingdom of Great Britain and Northern Ireland |
| HAA-HAZ | Hungary (Republic of) |
| HBA-HBZ | Switzerland (Confederation of) |
| HCA-HDZ | Ecuador |
| HEA-HEZ | Switzerland (Confederation of) |
| HFA-HFZ | Poland (Republic of) |
| HGA-HGZ | Hungary (Republic of) |
| HHA-HHZ | Haiti (Republic of) |
| HIA-HIZ | Dominican Republic |
| HJA-HKZ | Colombia (Republic of) |
| HLA-HLZ | Korea (Republic of) |
| HMA-HMZ | Democratic People's Republic of Korea |
| HNA-HNZ | Iraq (Republic of) |
| HOA-HPZ | Panama (Republic of) |
| HQA-HRZ | Honduras (Republic of) |
| HSA-HSZ | Thailand |
| HTA-HTZ | Nicaragua |
| HUA-HUZ | El Salvador (Republic of) |
| HVA-HVZ | Vatican City State |
| HWA-HYZ | France |
| HZA-HZZ | Saudi Arabia (Kingdom of) |
| H2A-H2Z | Cyprus (Republic of) |
| H3A-H3Z | Panama (Republic of) |
| H4A-H4Z | Solomon Islands |
| H6A-H7Z | Nicaragua |
| H8A-H9Z | Panama (Republic of) |
| IAA-IZZ | Italy |
| JAA-JSZ | Japan |
| JTA-JVZ | Mongolia |
| JWA-JXZ | Norway |
| JYA-JYZ | Jordan (Hashemite Kingdom of) |
| JZA-JZZ | Indonesia (Republic of) |
| J2A-J2Z | Djibouti (Republic of) |
| J3A-J3Z | Grenada |
| J4A-J4Z | Greece |
| J5A-J5Z | Guinea-Bissau (Republic of) |
| J6A-J6Z | Saint Lucia |
| J7A-J7Z | Dominica (Commonwealth of) |

| | |
|---|---|
| J8A-J8Z | Saint Vincent and the Grenadines |
| **KAA-KZZ** | **United States of America** |
| LAA-LNZ | Norway |
| LOA-LWZ | Argentine Republic |
| LXA-LXZ | Luxembourg |
| LYA-LYZ | Lithuania (Republic of) |
| LZA-LZZ | Bulgaria (Republic of) |
| L2A-L9Z | Argentine Republic |
| MAA-MZZ | United Kingdom of Great Britain and Northern Ireland |
| **NAA-NZZ** | **United States of America** |
| OAA-OCZ | Peru |
| ODA-ODZ | Lebanon |
| OEA-OEZ | Austria |
| OFA-OJZ | Finland |
| OKA-OLZ | Czech Republic |
| OMA-OMZ | Slovak Republic |
| ONA-OTZ | Belgium |
| OUA-OZZ | Denmark |
| PAA-PIZ | Netherlands (Kingdom of the) |
| PJA-PJZ | Netherlands (Kingdom of the) - Netherlands Antilles |
| PKA-POZ | Indonesia (Republic of) |
| PPA-PYZ | Brazil (Federative Republic of) |
| PZA-PZZ | Suriname (Republic of) |
| P2A-P2Z | Papua New Guinea |
| P3A-P3Z | Cyprus (Republic of) |
| P4A-P4Z | Netherlands (Kingdom of the) - Aruba |
| P5A-P9Z | Democratic People's Republic of Korea |
| RAA-RZZ | Russian Federation |
| SAA-SMZ | Sweden |
| SNA-SRZ | Poland (Republic of) |
| SSA-SSM | Egypt (Arab Republic of) |
| SSN-STZ | Sudan (Republic of the) |
| SUA-SUZ | Egypt (Arab Republic of) |
| SVA-SZZ | Greece |
| S2A-S3Z | Bangladesh (People's Republic of) |
| S5A-S5Z | Slovenia (Republic of) |
| S6A-S6Z | Singapore (Republic of) |
| S7A-S7Z | Seychelles (Republic of) |
| S8A-S8Z | South Africa (Republic of) |
| S9A-S9Z | Sao Tome and Principe (Democratic Republic of) |
| TAA-TCZ | Turkey |
| TDA-TDZ | Guatemala (Republic of) |
| TEA-TEZ | Costa Rica |
| TFA-TFZ | Iceland |
| TGA-TGZ | Guatemala (Republic of) |

| | |
|---|---|
| THA-THZ | France |
| TIA-TIZ | Costa Rica |
| TJA-TJZ | Cameroon (Republic of) |
| TKA-TKZ | France |
| TLA-TLZ | Central African Republic |
| TMA-TMZ | France |
| TNA-TNZ | Congo (Republic of the) |
| TOA-TQZ | France |
| TRA-TRZ | Gabonese Republic |
| TSA-TSZ | Tunisia |
| TTA-TTZ | Chad (Republic of) |
| TUA-TUZ | Côte d'Ivoire (Republic of) |
| TVA-TXZ | France |
| TYA-TYZ | Benin (Republic of) |
| TZA-TZZ | Mali (Republic of) |
| T2A-T2Z | Tuvalu |
| T3A-T3Z | Kiribati (Republic of) |
| T4A-T4Z | Cuba |
| T5A-T5Z | Somali Democratic Republic |
| T6A-T6Z | Afghanistan (Islamic State of) |
| T7A-T7Z | San Marino (Republic of) |
| T8A-T8Z | Palau (Republic of) |
| UAA-UIZ | Russian Federation |
| UJA-UMZ | Uzbekistan (Republic of) |
| UNA-UQZ | Kazakhstan (Republic of) |
| URA-UZZ | Ukraine |
| VAA-VGZ | Canada |
| VHA-VNZ | Australia |
| VOA-VOZ | Canada |
| VPA-VQZ | United Kingdom of Great Britain and Northern Ireland |
| VRA-VRZ | China (People's Republic of) - Hong Kong |
| VSA-VSZ | United Kingdom of Great Britain and Northern Ireland |
| VTA-VWZ | India (Republic of) |
| VXA-VYZ | Canada |
| VZA-VZZ | Australia |
| V2A-V2Z | Antigua and Barbuda |
| V3A-V3Z | Belize |
| V4A-V4Z | Saint Kitts and Nevis |
| V5A-V5Z | Namibia (Republic of) |
| V6A-V6Z | Micronesia (Federated States of) |
| V7A-V7Z | Marshall Islands (Republic of the) |
| V8A-V8Z | Brunei Darussalam |
| **WAA-WZZ** | **United States of America** |
| XAA-XIZ | Mexico |
| XJA-XOZ | Canada |

| | |
|---|---|
| XPA-XPZ | Denmark |
| XQA-XRZ | Chile |
| XSA-XSZ | China (People's Republic of) |
| XTA-XTZ | Burkina Faso |
| XUA-XUZ | Cambodia (Kingdom of) |
| XVA-XVZ | Viet Nam (Socialist Republic of) |
| XWA-XWZ | Lao People's Democratic Republic |
| XXA-XXZ | China (People's Republic of) - Macao (WRC-07) |
| XYA-XZZ | Myanmar (Union of) |
| YAA-YAZ | Afghanistan (Islamic State of) |
| YBA-YHZ | Indonesia (Republic of) |
| YIA-YIZ | Iraq (Republic of) |
| YJA-YJZ | Vanuatu (Republic of) |
| YKA-YKZ | Syrian Arab Republic |
| YLA-YLZ | Latvia (Republic of) |
| YMA-YMZ | Turkey |
| YNA-YNZ | Nicaragua |
| YOA-YRZ | Romania |
| YSA-YSZ | El Salvador (Republic of) |
| YTA-YUZ | Serbia (Republic of) (WRC-07) |
| YVA-YYZ | Venezuela (Republic of) |
| Y2A-Y9Z | Germany (Federal Republic of) |
| ZAA-ZAZ | Albania (Republic of) |
| ZBA-ZJZ | United Kingdom of Great Britain and Northern Ireland |
| ZKA-ZMZ | New Zealand |
| ZNA-ZOZ | United Kingdom of Great Britain and Northern Ireland |
| ZPA-ZPZ | Paraguay (Republic of) |
| ZQA-ZQZ | United Kingdom of Great Britain and Northern Ireland |
| ZRA-ZUZ | South Africa (Republic of) |
| ZVA-ZZZ | Brazil (Federative Republic of) |
| Z2A-Z2Z | Zimbabwe (Republic of) |
| Z3A-Z3Z | The Former Yugoslav Republic of Macedonia |
| 2AA-2ZZ | United Kingdom of Great Britain and Northern Ireland |
| 3AA-3AZ | Monaco (Principality of) |
| 3BA-3BZ | Mauritius (Republic of) |
| 3CA-3CZ | Equatorial Guinea (Republic of) |
| 3DA-3DM | Swaziland (Kingdom of) |
| 3DN-3DZ | Fiji (Republic of) |
| 3EA-3FZ | Panama (Republic of) |
| 3GA-3GZ | Chile |
| 3HA-3UZ | China (People's Republic of) |
| 3VA-3VZ | Tunisia |
| 3WA-3WZ | Viet Nam (Socialist Republic of) |
| 3XA-3XZ | Guinea (Republic of) |
| 3YA-3YZ | Norway |

| | |
|---|---|
| 3ZA-3ZZ | Poland (Republic of) |
| 4AA-4CZ | Mexico |
| 4DA-4IZ | Philippines (Republic of the) |
| 4JA-4KZ | Azerbaijani Republic |
| 4LA-4LZ | Georgia (Republic of) |
| 4MA-4MZ | Venezuela (Republic of) |
| 4OA-4OZ | Montenegro (Republic of) (WRC-07) |
| 4PA-4SZ | Sri Lanka (Democratic Socialist Republic of) |
| 4TA-4TZ | Peru |
| 4UA-4UZ | United Nations |
| 4VA-4VZ | Haiti (Republic of) |
| 4WA-4WZ | Democratic Republic of Timor-Leste (WRC-03) |
| 4XA-4XZ | Israel (State of) |
| 4YA-4YZ | International Civil Aviation Organization |
| 4ZA-4ZZ | Israel (State of) |
| 5AA-5AZ | Libya (Socialist People's Libyan Arab Jamahiriya) |
| 5BA-5BZ | Cyprus (Republic of) |
| 5CA-5GZ | Morocco (Kingdom of) |
| 5HA-5IZ | Tanzania (United Republic of) |
| 5JA-5KZ | Colombia (Republic of) |
| 5LA-5MZ | Liberia (Republic of) |
| 5NA-5OZ | Nigeria (Federal Republic of) |
| 5PA-5QZ | Denmark |
| 5RA-5SZ | Madagascar (Republic of) |
| 5TA-5TZ | Mauritania (Islamic Republic of) |
| 5UA-5UZ | Niger (Republic of the) |
| 5VA-5VZ | Togolese Republic |
| 5WA-5WZ | Samoa (Independent State of) |
| 5XA-5XZ | Uganda (Republic of) |
| 5YA-5ZZ | Kenya (Republic of) |
| 6AA-6BZ | Egypt (Arab Republic of) |
| 6CA-6CZ | Syrian Arab Republic |
| 6DA-6JZ | Mexico |
| 6KA-6NZ | Korea (Republic of) |
| 6OA-6OZ | Somali Democratic Republic |
| 6PA-6SZ | Pakistan (Islamic Republic of) |
| 6TA-6UZ | Sudan (Republic of the) |
| 6VA-6WZ | Senegal (Republic of) |
| 6XA-6XZ | Madagascar (Republic of) |
| 6YA-6YZ | Jamaica |
| 6ZA-6ZZ | Liberia (Republic of) |
| 7AA-7IZ | Indonesia (Republic of) |
| 7JA-7NZ | Japan |
| 7OA-7OZ | Yemen (Republic of) |
| 7PA-7PZ | Lesotho (Kingdom of) |

| | |
|---|---|
| 7QA-7QZ | Malawi |
| 7RA-7RZ | Algeria (People's Democratic Republic of) |
| 7SA-7SZ | Sweden |
| 7TA-7YZ | Algeria (People's Democratic Republic of) |
| 7ZA-7ZZ | Saudi Arabia (Kingdom of) |
| 8AA-8IZ | Indonesia (Republic of) |
| 8JA-8NZ | Japan |
| 8OA-8OZ | Botswana (Republic of) |
| 8PA-8PZ | Barbados |
| 8QA-8QZ | Maldives (Republic of) |
| 8RA-8RZ | Guyana |
| 8SA-8SZ | Sweden |
| 8TA-8YZ | India (Republic of) |
| 8ZA-8ZZ | Saudi Arabia (Kingdom of) |
| 9AA-9AZ | Croatia (Republic of) |
| 9BA-9DZ | Iran (Islamic Republic of) |
| 9EA-9FZ | Ethiopia (Federal Democratic Republic of) |
| 9GA-9GZ | Ghana |
| 9HA-9HZ | Malta |
| 9IA-9JZ | Zambia (Republic of) |
| 9KA-9KZ | Kuwait (State of) |
| 9LA-9LZ | Sierra Leone |
| 9MA-9MZ | Malaysia |
| 9NA-9NZ | Nepal |
| 9OA-9TZ | Democratic Republic of the Congo |
| 9UA-9UZ | Burundi (Republic of) |
| 9VA-9VZ | Singapore (Republic of) |
| 9WA-9WZ | Malaysia |
| 9XA-9XZ | Rwandese Republic |
| 9YA-9ZZ | Trinidad and Tobago |

**Third-Party Communications and Amateur Radio**

If all of this information about ham radios is somewhat intimidating, do not despair. "You" can still use ham radios for communications without being a licensed operator. Yes, you do have to have a ham license in order to legally transmit by ham equipment (or be under the direct supervision of someone else who is licensed), but there is an alternative – third-party communication.

Third-party communications occur when a licensed operator sends either written or verbal messages on behalf of unlicensed persons or organizations. There are two "controls" on third-party communication.

First, the communication must be noncommercial and of a personal nature. Asking a ham operator to contact another ham operator located in an area just hit by tornados and, because of being without power, phones do not work in Grandma Sally's city so you can check up on her, is okay. Asking a ham to send a message out that you have an old Chevy for sale would not be okay.

Second, the message must be going to a permitted area. Transmitting from a US location to another US location is okay, but transmitting from the US to another country may not. Because third-party communications bypass a country's normal telephone and postal systems, many foreign governments forbid such communications. In order to transmit from one country to another, the other country must have signed a third-party agreement with the US. What follows is a list of those countries that do have third-party a communications agreement with the US.

| V2 | Antigua / Barbuda |
| --- | --- |
| LU | Argentina |
| VK | Australia |
| V3 | Belize |
| CP | Bolivia |
| T9 | Bosnia-Herzegovina |
| PY | Brazil |
| VE | Canada |
| CE | Chile |
| HK | Colombia |
| D6 | Comoros (Federal Islamic Republic of) |
| TI | Costa Rica |
| CO | Cuba |
| HI | Dominican Republic |
| J7 | Dominica |
| HC | Ecuador |
| YS | El Salvador |
| C5 | Gambia, The |
| 9G | Ghana |
| J3 | Grenada |
| TG | Guatemala |
| 8R | Guyana |
| HH | Haiti |
| HR | Honduras |
| 4X | Israel |
| 6Y | Jamaica |
| JY | Jordan |
| EL | Liberia |
| V7 | Marshall Islands |
| XE | Mexico |
| V6 | Micronesia, Federated States of |
| YN | Nicaragua |
| HP | Panama |

| | |
|---|---|
| ZP | Paraguay |
| OA | Peru |
| DU | Philippines |
| VR6 | Pitcairn Island |
| V4 | St. Christopher / Nevis |
| J6 | St. Lucia |
| J8 | St. Vincent and the Grenadines |
| 9L | Sierra Leone |
| ZS | South Africa |
| 3DA | Swaziland |
| 9Y | Trinidad / Tobago |
| TA | Turkey |
| GB | United Kingdom |
| CX | Uruguay |
| YV | Venezuela |
| 4U1ITUITU | Geneva |
| 4U1VICVIC | Vienna |

Remember, before TSHTF, keep your pantry well stocked, your powder dry, and your batteries fully charged. 73

# APPENDIX A

**American Radio Relay League**

**Affiliated Amateur Radio Clubs in**

**North Dakota**

**ARRL Affiliated Club**   Hawksnest Repeater Association
City:                      Cathay, ND
Call Sign:                 K0ATK
Section:                   ND

**ARRL Affiliated Club**   Pembina County Amateur Radio Club, Inc
City:                      Cavalier, ND
Call Sign:                 N0CAV
Section:                   ND

**ARRL Affiliated Club**   Theodore Roosevelt Amateur Radio Club
City:                      Dickinson, ND
Call Sign:                 K0ND
Section:                   ND
Links:                     www.qsl.net/k0alv

**ARRL Affiliated Club**   Red River Radio Amateurs, Inc.
City:                      Fargo, ND
Call Sign:                 W0ILO
Section:                   ND
Links:                     www.rrra.org

**ARRL Affiliated Club**   North Dakota State University
City:                      Fargo, ND
Call Sign:                 W0HSC
Section:                   ND
Links:                     www.w0hsc.ndsu.nodak.edu

**ARRL Affiliated Club**   Forx Amateur Radio Club
City:                      Grand Forks, ND
Call Sign:                 WA0JXT
Section:                   ND
Links:                     www.qsl.net/wa0jxt, wa0jxt.org

**ARRL Special Service Club** North Dakota Radio Association
City:                      Minot, ND
Call Sign:                 K0LN
Section:                   ND
Links:                     http://k0ln.com

**ARRL Affiliated Club**   Souris Valley Amateur Radio Club
City:                      Minot, ND
Call Sign:                 K0AJW
Section:                   ND
Links:                     www.qsl.net/svarc/new.htm

**ARRL Affiliated Club**      Three Rivers Amateur Radio Club
**City:**      Wahpeton, ND
**Call Sign:**      W0END
**Section:**      ND
**Links:**      w0end.tripod.com/

# APPENDIX B

# Amateur Radio License Holders

# in

# North Dakota
# (by City)

## FCC Amateur Radio Licenses in Abercrombie

WB0RQP
Lois M Myhre
Box 124
Abercrombie ND 58001

WB0RRG
Steven L Myhre
Box 124
Abercrombie ND 58001

WB0WRN
Owen S Myhre
Box 124
Abercrombie ND 58001

WA0RWM
Lois A Jorgensen
Box 55
Abercrombie ND 58001

WA0VGJ
Gerald L Jorgensen
Box 55
Abercrombie ND 58001

WB0ITM
Barbara A Myhre
Abercrombie ND 58001

## FCC Amateur Radio Licenses in Absaraka

KC0QXF
Todd D Meyer
117 Main St
Absaraka ND 58002

## FCC Amateur Radio Licenses in Alamo

WA0HAD
Melvin I Wisdahl

Hcr 2 Box 54
Alamo ND 58830

W0BLQ
Olav C Egge
215 S Tallman
Alamo ND 58830

## FCC Amateur Radio Licenses in Anamoose

N7OTF
Marino L Linardon Sr
Anamoose ND 58710

## FCC Amateur Radio Licenses in Aneta

KA0CVT
James C Larsgaard
Rr 1 Box 28
Aneta ND 58212

W0ZVL
La Verne D Solberg
Rr 1 Box 32
Aneta ND 582129710

KA0KTG
Adolph R Kjar
Box 337
Aneta ND 58212

KB2ZFC
Jeremiah J Miller
RR 1
Aneta ND 58212

W0ZVN
Perry C Sather
168 Serns Ave
Aneta ND 58212

W0FVX
Quinten L Haraldson

Aneta ND 58212

KB0VCR
Alfred L Borah
Aneta ND 58212

## FCC Amateur Radio Licenses in Antler

KB0SAC
Kirk W Preskey
10165 29th Ave NW
Antler ND 58711

## FCC Amateur Radio Licenses in Ardoch

KC0ODC
Suzanne H Schmidt
3416 24th St NE
Ardoch ND 58213

KB0DQU
Douglas D Praska
207 Wall St
Ardoch ND 58261

## FCC Amateur Radio Licenses in Argusville

KB0HNQ
Teresa M Ohnstad
17270 20th St
Argusville ND 58005

KB0BRY
Kevin J Ohnstad
17270 20th St SE
Argusville ND 58005

## FCC Amateur Radio Licenses in Arthur

KB0FGR

Timothy W Rand
PO Box 53
Arthur ND 580060053

N0HUU
Hans G Wallin Jr
Arthur ND 580060125

## FCC Amateur Radio Licenses in Arvilla

KD0OMJ
Edwin E Schulz
3291 21st Ave NE
Arvilla ND 58214

KF0JP
Charles N Knudson
3323 22nd Ave NE
Arvilla ND 58214

N0NYR
Ruth E Wilson
3323 22nd Ave NE
Arvilla ND 58214

N0YUX
Peter C Haugen
2125 33rd St NE
Arvilla ND 58214

KA0HQO
Terry L Petsinger
Rr 1 Box 83
Arvilla ND 58214

WB0JGM
Bonnie J Stiles
2927 US Hwy 2
Arvilla ND 58214

## FCC Amateur Radio Licenses in Ashley

KD0RER

James W Grossmann
Ashley ND 58413

N2GFA
Gerard R Zlotkowski
Ashley ND 584130539

---

**FCC Amateur Radio Licenses in
Baldwin**

KG6JP
Gary L Vennie
24051 12th St NE
Baldwin ND 58521

---

**FCC Amateur Radio Licenses in
Bantry**

WA0UOK
Richard R Willoughby
7808 3rd Ave N
Bantry ND 58713

---

**FCC Amateur Radio Licenses in
Barney**

KC0RYD
Robert A Ulvestad
210 Iowa Ave
Barney ND 58008

KA7SSI
Robert A Ulvestad
210 Iowa Ave
Barney ND 58008

KC0KEV
Robert A Ulvestad
210 Iowa Ave
Barney ND 58008

---

**FCC Amateur Radio Licenses in
Bathgate**

KB0EQY
Donald E Wert
Rt 1 Box 38
Bathgate ND 58216

KB0EQZ
Deborah S Wert
Rt 1 Box 38
Bathgate ND 58216

---

**FCC Amateur Radio Licenses in
Beach**

KC0UDM
Kitty J Knapkewicz
316 2nd St SE
Beach ND 58621

K0WND
Kitty J Knapkewicz
316 2nd St SE
Beach ND 58621

K0DLW
Daniel L Walz
202 8th St NW
Beach ND 58621

KB0VSC
Joseph C Michels
672 Black Diamond Rd
Beach ND 586219670

K0WND
Gerald A Knapkewicz
Beach ND 58621

K0AJH
A J Hamilton
Beach ND 586210099

KC0UDK
Judy F Hamilton
Beach ND 58621

KC0UDL
James P Zielsdorf
Beach ND 58621

W0ZKE
James P Zielsdorf
Beach ND 58621

W0III
E K Hamilton
Beach ND 586210099

KC0CVH
Carl D Strum
Beach ND 586210516

AB0KS
Carl D Strum
Beach ND 586210516

## FCC Amateur Radio Licenses in Belcourt

N0ZXA
James L Haley
Belcourt ND 58316

## FCC Amateur Radio Licenses in Belfield

W0RTK
Clarence C Thompson
129 N Main St
Belfield ND 586220068

WD0CWN
Curtis H Molm
Box 59 Rr 3
Belfield ND 58622

KD0DDF
Corinne E Krauss
Belfield ND 58622

## FCC Amateur Radio Licenses in Bergen

N0EK
Edward A Kasprowicz
212 Townsend St
Bergen ND 58792

## FCC Amateur Radio Licenses in Berthold

KE7LD
Leroy C Thompson
Box 97
Berthold ND 58718

N7KMP
Phyllis A Thompson
Box 97
Berthold ND 58718

## FCC Amateur Radio Licenses in Beulah

KB0MII
Steven R Larson
500 3rd Ave NW
Beulah ND 58523

KB0QHX
Jared C Allar
1701 6th Ave NE
Beulah ND 58523

KB0YBW
Karen M Allar
1701 6th Ave NE
Beulah ND 58523

KF0ON
Connie J Allar
1901 6th Ave NE
Beulah ND 58523

K0GWP

Gustav Morlock
Box 94
Beulah ND 58523

## FCC Amateur Radio Licenses in Binford

KB0TIZ
Owen E Dramstad
155 102nd Ave NE
Binford ND 58416

N0SKO
James A Dramstad
155 102nd Ave NE
Binford ND 58416

W0ORU
Bjarne M Dramstad
Box 68
Binford ND 58416

KB0AMP
Jill R Mains
R Rt 1 Box 69
Binford ND 58416

KA0TXU
Dorreen M Beaver
101 Broad St
Binford ND 58416

KB0OCB
Linda Spafford
114 Charles Ave
Binford ND 58416

WM0J
Frederick T Spafford
114 Charles Ave
Binford ND 58416

WI0A
Loren A Dramstad
10241 Hwy 200
Binford ND 58416

N0OTO
Dennis R Becherl
307 Miller Ave W
Binford ND 58416

KA0VWN
Delphine E Beaver
Binford ND 58416

WB0I
Kevin M Beaver
Binford ND 58416

KC0RZM
Karen E Becherl
Binford ND 58416

N0VKI
Sherman Rorvig
Binford ND 584160225

## FCC Amateur Radio Licenses in Bismark

KB0OCP
Darrell P Lieux
1805 110 Ave NE
Bismarck ND 58501

KB0SBY
Jarrod C Lieux
1805 110 Ave NE
Bismarck ND 58501

KB0NCU
Eric P Lieux
1805 110th Ave NE
Bismarck ND 58501

KB0OCQ
Melody L Lieux
1805 110th Ave NE
Bismarck ND 58501

KC0WCK
Steven W Clayton
4290 78th Ave NE
Bismarck ND 58503

KB0WBM
Karl C Venneberg
800 79th Ave NE
Bismarck ND 58501

K0DWX
Laurence S Colebank
742 Albany Dr
Bismarck ND 585046541

KD0QBZ
Richard R Solberg
9252 Apple Creek Rd
Bismarck ND 58504

KC0RYH
William S Okrepkie
512 Augsburg Ave
Bismarck ND 58504

KC0PGB
Robert L Eriksen
706 Augsburg Ave
Bismarck ND 58504

KC0PGD
Matthew H Eriksen
706 Augsburg Ave
Bismarck ND 58504

WA0HHI
William P Pearce
204 Ave B W
Bismarck ND 58501

KC0RKN
Kathleen M Pace
404 Ave C E
Bismarck ND 58501

K0QZE
Charles D Grumbo
419 Ave C W
Bismarck ND 58501

W0IKW
Thomas B Grothe
2128 Ave E
Bismarck ND 58501

KC0RUB
Alex H Walth
241 Boeing Ave
Bismarck ND 58504

N0IIR
Chad A Wachter
2126 Boston Dr
Bismarck ND 58504

KB0IUZ
Sheldon R Babeck
Rr 1 Box 289B
Bismarck ND 58501

N3BIM
David C Jensen
Box 357
Bismarck ND 58502

N0IPC
Delbert D Kastner
Box 456
Bismarck ND 58502

WD0CJJ
Rocky L Hefty
8617 Briardale Drive
Bismarck ND 585043057

KB0VOC
James R Fors
431 Browning Ave
Bismarck ND 58501

N0ASB
Robert L Francis
209 Cheyenne Ave
Bismarck ND 58501

KC0HSO
Ardella M Miller
3010 Clairmont Rd
Bismarck ND 58503

KB0RX
Delbert J Thompson
2905 Clover Ln
Bismarck ND 58503

N0JLY
David M Muggli
820 Cody Dr
Bismarck ND 58503

KC0EIQ
John A Schneider
1633 Cologne Dr
Bismarck ND 58504

KC0ZDO
Brian R Messmer
2606 Colonial Dr
Bismarck ND 58503

N0RYI
Dennis T Tiedman
1612 Columbia Dr
Bismarck ND 58504

N0TKR
John A Lacher
234 Connecticut St
Bismarck ND 58504

KD0ECR
Gregory S Peterson
1829 Constitution Dr
Bismarck ND 58501

N0VST
Justin W Bohn
1872 Contessa Dr
Bismarck ND 58501

N0YMZ
William J Heuther
1715 Country W Rd
Bismarck ND 58501

KC0MNF
Leroy T Miller
1500 Countryside Drive
Bismarck ND 58501

N0NTN
W Kendall Johnson
1003 Crescent Ln
Bismarck ND 58501

KC0JYM
Steven L Anderson
7650 Dogwood Drive
Bismarck ND 585043051

N0HEB
Galeila G Schauer
524 Dohn Ave
Bismarck ND 585031010

N0XLZ
Robby L Heupel
4330 Drake Dr
Bismarck ND 58503

W0JQH
Ernest J Vold
606 E Columbia Dr
Bismarck ND 58501

N0WKB
Howard Burns Jr
422 E Denver Ave
Bismarck ND 58504

KD0DDQ
Aaron E Campbell
1502 E Ave E3
Bismarck ND 58501

KB0OCN
Richard A Storhaug
1325 E Boulevard Ave
Bismarck ND 58501

KB0OCO
Matthew W Storhaug
1325 E Boulevard Ave
Bismarck ND 58501

NT0U
Rodney A Storhaug
1325 E Boulevard Ave
Bismarck ND 58501

WB0FDY
Allen R Wetzel
1615 E Capitol Ave 4
Bismarck ND 58501

W0CZM
Larry E Bushey
1818 E Capitol Ave Apt 302
Bismarck ND 58501

KB0QYZ
Margaret Schempp
409 E Central Ave
Bismarck ND 58501

WA0HPN
Gerald L Schempp
409 E Central Ave
Bismarck ND 585011856

KC0IMA
Dosch-Schempp Amateur Radio Club
409 E Central Ave
Bismarck ND 585011856

W0TSL
Dosch-Schempp Amateur Radio Club
409 E Central Ave
Bismarck ND 585011856

KC0OXW
Benjamin L Towner
510 E Central Ave
Bismarck ND 58501

N0HGO
Joan T Storhaug
518 E Columbia Dr
Bismarck ND 58504

N0IIA
Richard J Smith
2612 E Divide
Bismarck ND 58501

W0CTS
Joseph L Mader
1520 E Divide Ave
Bismarck ND 58501

W0AZN
Kenneth J Ekblad
1724 E Divide Ave
Bismarck ND 58501

N0XMR
John D Wehmhoefer
209 E Edmonton Dr
Bismarck ND 58501

W0ZJZ
James P Murdoch
1223 E Highland Acres Rd
Bismarck ND 58501

KD0QBX
Anthony E Rohrich
1020 E Indiana Ave
Bismarck ND 58504

KB0QYS
Janell S Quinlan
3823 E Princeton Ave
Bismarck ND 58504

KA3FWR
Curtis G Smith
3837 E Regent Dr
Bismarck ND 58501

AC5QL
Todd Dixon
1321 Eagles View Place
Bismarck ND 58503

KC0ZWR
Robert J Roswick
4315 England St
Bismarck ND 58504

K0RJR
Robert J Roswick
4315 England St
Bismarck ND 58504

KB0IUY
Edward M Babeck
2724 Essex Loop
Bismarck ND 58504

KB0UK
Bruce B Skogen
107 Estevan Dr
Bismarck ND 58501

N0DJE
Barbara A Skogen
107 Estevan Dr
Bismarck ND 58501

AB1CM
Theodore T Poppke
234 Estevan Dr
Bismarck ND 58503

KB0YLU
John P Martin
5654 Falconer Dr
Bismarck ND 58504

N0NRQ
Steven W Krein
9507 Forest Dr
Bismarck ND 58503

KC0VRY
Justin D Walsh
9610 Forest Dr
Bismarck ND 58503

N0ZNS
Olmstead W Adams
3039 Greenwood Dr
Bismarck ND 58501

KA0NUJ
Mark G Schulz
2062 Grimsrud Dr
Bismarck ND 58501

KB0LFB
Shawn J Schulz
2062 Grimsrud Dr
Bismarck ND 58501

WB0VGG
Glenn R Schulz
2062 Grimsrud Dr
Bismarck ND 58501

KA0NUI
Shirley D Schulz
2062 Grimsruddr
Bismarck ND 58501

KC0RTY
John T Reynolds
3334 Hackberry St
Bismarck ND 58503

KC0RTZ
Keri A Reynolds
3334 Hackberry St
Bismarck ND 58503

KC0RUX
Dawn A Reynolds
3334 Hackberry St
Bismarck ND 58503

KC0RUY
Ryan W Reynolds
3334 Hackberry St
Bismarck ND 58503

N0YCV
Wayne G Sease
2223 Harding Ave
Bismarck ND 58501

KC0MNH
Mark E Schmidt
4605 Hay Creek Dr
Bismarck ND 58503

KC0MNI
Alex M Schmidt
4605 Hay Creek Dr
Bismarck ND 58503

KC0MXG
Wayne A Sellner
3507 Heartland Loop
Bismarck ND 585038995

N5RJR
Kent C Martin
2507 Henry St
Bismarck ND 58503

W0HS
Bruce F Mc Collom
7115 Hightop Ln
Bismarck ND 585021014

KC0RUA
Jeff M Horan
1111 Hillside Terrace
Bismarck ND 58501

N0YCU
Joseph J Kalvoda
2912 Homestead Dr
Bismarck ND 58501

WB0ATB
Howard Burns
2508 Hoover Ave
Bismarck ND 58501

KC7MRW
Harlyn A Wetzel
8365 Irish Ln
Bismarck ND 58504

KB6L
Robert J Litt
3000 Ithica Dr
Bismarck ND 58503

KD0MMC
Zachary S Heinert
3211 Jericho Rd
Bismarck ND 58503

KD0ZSH
Zachary S Heinert
3211 Jericho Rd
Bismarck ND 58503

K0ZSH
Zachary S Heinert
3357 Jericho Rd
Bismarck ND 58503

KE5WJE
Keith E Lesser
3841 Jericho Rd Apt 3
Bismarck ND 58503

N0MBE
Richard A Ziegler
514 Jumper Dr
Bismarck ND 585030252

KC0MNE
Karen K Williams
514 Juniper Dr
Bismarck ND 58503

KC0PAE
Aaron J Fettig
801 Juniper Pl
Bismarck ND 58503

KF0DL
Peter J Fettig
801 Juniper Pl
Bismarck ND 585030190

KA0NUB
George L Struchynski
9720 Kelly Dr
Bismarck ND 585019701

WA0VHQ
Matt J Kronberger
316 Laredo Dr
Bismarck ND 58504

N0HYT
Lynn T Oby
7500 Lariat Ln
Bismarck ND 585019122

KB0EBB
John A Larson
3340 Larson Rd
Bismarck ND 58504

KB0ZUH
William A Abeling
1756 Lilac Ln
Bismarck ND 58501

KC0WCL
Kyle P Hagen
1036 Lincoln Ave
Bismarck ND 58504

KC0AIT
Kathleen L Schaan
9001 Lincoln Rd
Bismarck ND 58504

KC0CIX
Matthew D Summers
316 Lunar Ln
Bismarck ND 58501

ND0S
North Dakota Frequently Active Rad
Telegraphrs
316 Lunar Ln
Bismarck ND 58501

KC0NDC
Andrew T Turman
525 Macon Dr
Bismarck ND 58504

KC0PIC
Bismarck Bsa Troop 11
690 Macon Dr
Bismarck ND 58504

WA0BSA
Bismarck Bsa Troop 11
690 Macon Dr
Bismarck ND 58504

N0FAZ
Mark A Malm
690 Macon Dr
Bismarck ND 58504

N0HGR
Sharon R Malm
690 Macon Dr

Bismarck ND 58504

KC0ILL
Alex J Malm
690 Macon Dr
Bismarck ND 58504

KC0HKQ
John A Birdzell
1023 Mandan St
Bismarck ND 58501

WU0D
Arta C Leno
1201 Mandan St
Bismarck ND 58501

K0TN
Gilbert V Nordstrom
1708 Marian Dr
Bismarck ND 58501

WB0VLF
Daniel A Nordstrom
1708 Marian Drive
Bismarck ND 58501

KB0ZNY
Evelyn J Nordstrom
1708 Marion Dr
Bismarck ND 58501

W0CZR
Donald J Kostelecky
2000 Meadow Ridge Pl
Bismarck ND 58501

K0NZ
Donald J Kostelecky
2000 Meadow Ridge Place
Bismarck ND 58501

KB0RLW
Martin D Carpenter
1509 Michigan Ave

Bismarck ND 58504

WB0SUS
Daniel J Crothers
1717 Montego Drive
Bismarck ND 58503

KE4KPQ
Lewis N Cunningham
1747 Montego Drive
Bismarck ND 58503

KD0FYC
Marvin D Shaw
3513 Montreal St
Bismarck ND 58503

NT0S
Richard A Storhaug
3221 Montreal St Apt 11
Bismarck ND 585030426

KB0MTJ
Dave B Holden
1801 N 17th St
Bismarck ND 58501

N0ZNT
Howard J Walth
1827 N 20th St
Bismarck ND 58501

KB0ZZR
Bonnie Tunnicliff Johnson
2029 N 2nd St
Bismarck ND 58501

KB0ZZS
Christopher L Johnson
2029 N 2nd St
Bismarck ND 58501

KC0ZWP
Daren J Repnow
921 N Griffin St

Bismarck ND 58501

K9FQO
Derek Oldenburger
1208 N Parkview Dr
Bismarck ND 58501

W0OSP
John E Stiles
4008 N Valley Loop
Bismarck ND 58503

N0SXY
Ryan D Schweitzer
2030 N Washington St  Apt 5
Bismarck ND 58504

K0DFF
Thomas J Fitzsimmons
614 N 11th St
Bismarck ND 585014148

KB0ADX
Raymond A Myers
925 N 11th St
Bismarck ND 58501

N0ZKF
Merle E Rutschke
1941 N 11th St 1
Bismarck ND 58501

KB0IVR
Mary J Haux
619.5 N 12th St
Bismarck ND 58501

KA0KZY
Ronald A Swanson
912 N 13th
Bismarck ND 58501

KB0MTH
Gerald A Carman
501 N 13th St

Bismarck ND 58501

N0HGP
Rebecca L Dosch
1112 N 13th St
Bismarck ND 58501

N0HGQ
James J Dosch
1112 N 13th St
Bismarck ND 58501

N0CYK
Lorne D Campbell
718 N 13th St
Bismarck ND 58501

KB0LEZ
Steven J Dosch
1112 N 13th St N
Bismarck ND 58501

KD0KPH
Wesley F Kudrna
1429 N 14th St
Bismarck ND 58501

K0BOT
Donald A Feimer
1919 N 14th St
Bismarck ND 58501

N0DJK
Arne S Loge
906 N 15th St
Bismarck ND 58501

KB0CHN
Timothy A Thorstenson
1012 N 16 St
Bismarck ND 58501

KC0UTU
Michael E Hancock
408 N 16th St

Bismarck ND 58501

K0HAN
Michael E Hancock
408 N 16th St
Bismarck ND 58501

WD0HTF
Glenn A Elliott
1321 N 16th St
Bismarck ND 58501

KD0NTJ
Reid A Forster
1504 N 16th St
Bismarck ND 58501

WD0HOO
Ronald A Poer
2013 N 16th St 4
Bismarck ND 58501

K0TVS
Patrick J Whitlock
2002 N 16th St Apt 1
Bismarck ND 58501

KB0EHT
George C Paraskeva
1504 N 18 St
Bismarck ND 58501

KC0WFC
Justin P Cremer
313 N 19th St
Bismarck ND 58501

W0LOL
Laurence S Engelman
612 N 19th St
Bismarck ND 58501

K0ALV
Rodney A Bakke
1601 N 19th St

Bismarck ND 58501

N0MBH
Jon G Barthel
4005 N 19th St 125
Bismarck ND 58503

KB0LDZ
Ben D Twingley
1960 N 20th St
Bismarck ND 58501

KB0BBC
Joseph F Steffen
700 N 22 St
Bismarck ND 58501

N0JMG
Merton A Johnsrud
1206 N 22 St
Bismarck ND 58501

WF0O
Clarence H Babcock
737 N 23rd St
Bismarck ND 58501

KG0LZ
Christopher B Runge
305 N 23rd St  118
Bismarck ND 58501

N0ZNU
Bradley J Thiel
419 N 24th St
Bismarck ND 58501

W0VAI
Harvey G Van Erem
1135 N 26th St
Bismarck ND 58501

KB0GJQ
Anne L Wham
1128 N 27th St

Bismarck ND 58501

N0RYE
Theodore R Stockert
1033 N 29th St
Bismarck ND 58501

KB0TSH
James E Haakedahl
1216.5 N 2nd St
Bismarck ND 58501

WB0SXC
Robert Arso
1930 N 2nd St
Bismarck ND 58501

KB0KDG
Kurt W Carufel
941 N 33 St
Bismarck ND 58501

KC0JYL
Curtis D Schorsch
830 N 35th
Bismarck ND 58501

KA0SNA
Mary B Struchynski
2040 N 3rd St
Bismarck ND 58501

K0CCA
George T Duemeland
215 N 3rd St
Bismarck ND 58501

KA0BUI
Paige A Newton
1322 N 4 St Apt 2
Bismarck ND 58501

W0GGR
Theodore M Thorson Sr
1304 N 4th St

Bismarck ND 58501

WA0MSJ
Robert J Mc Connell
1918 N 5th St
Bismarck ND 585011805

KB0MDK
Larry M Olson
1007 N 5th St 1
Bismarck ND 58501

WB0TDD
Bruce E Keller
1019 N 8th St
Bismarck ND 58501

KA0ETO
G Richard Veal
1829 N 8th St
Bismarck ND 58501

WB0WFE
Stanley H Haas
300 N Brandon Lp
Bismarck ND 58502

KC0OJB
Bill G Peters
805 N Griffin St
Bismarck ND 58501

KB0RCH
James J Erhart
405 N Hannifin
Bismarck ND 58501

KG4RFD
Steven T Takacs
504 N Hannifin St
Bismarck ND 58501

KC0UM
Roger D Bjerke
2427 N Washington St

Bismarck ND 58501

KD0PPN
Joshua C Lachenmeier
126 New Jersey St
Bismarck ND 58504

KC0HFV
Lawrene L Manthe
1305 Northview Ln
Bismarck ND 58501

AB0QI
Lawrene L Manthe
1305 Northview Ln
Bismarck ND 58501

K7MYH
Bruce N Vadnais
1814 Oakland Dr
Bismarck ND 58504

N0KUD
Linda K Vadnais
1814 Oakland Dr
Bismarck ND 58504

KA1ZNK
Jeff L Kramer
3001 Ohio St
Bismarck ND 58503

WA7GVT
Dennis W Howard
3504 Overlook Dr
Bismarck ND 585010261

N7HII
Ruth E Howard
3504 Overlook Drive
Bismarck ND 58503

KA0ZVF
Richard J Smith
901 Parkview Dr

Bismarck ND 585012466

N0WJN
Arin J Buringrud
438 Piccadilly Cir
Bismarck ND 58504

KC0MNR
Kyle W Becker
443 Piccadilly Circle
Bismarck ND 585047323

KB0VDY
Kenneth L Jarolimek
1519 Portland Dr
Bismarck ND 58504

K0JLU
Edward H Kubis
3824 Prairie Pines Loop
Bismarck ND 58503

KD0AAH
Rodney T Carpenter
3905 Prairie Pines Loop
Bismarck ND 58503

N8SQC
Charlene B Smith
1640 Prairie View Drive
Bismarck ND 58502

KC0BSO
Sean M Johnson
6405 Preston Loop
Bismarck ND 58504

KB0QZB
Paul D Meyers
133 Redstone Dr
Bismarck ND 58501

WB0SWW
Eugene R Elhard
1404 Richmond Dr

Bismarck ND 58501

N0YMC
Clinton E Grenz
1330 Ridgeview Ln
Bismarck ND 58501

KA0NYA
Oscar Kroll
945 River View Ave
Bismarck ND 58504

N0WVX
Michael P Estabrook
1030 Riverview Ave
Bismarck ND 58504

KB0ACP
Anthony Reisenauer
1116 Riverview Ave
Bismarck ND 58504

N0QCU
Kevin T Schneider
1306 Riverwood Dr
Bismarck ND 585046244

KB0JGX
Richard R Solberg
RR 2
Bismarck ND 58501

N0KDM
Kevin D Mahon
318 Rutland Dr
Bismarck ND 58504

KB0ZAA
Kevin D Mahon
318 Rutland Dr
Bismarck ND 58504

KB0RLT
Harold S Parkin
1720 Ryan Dr

Bismarck ND 58501

KB0TJK
Andrew H Parkin
1720 Ryan Dr
Bismarck ND 58501

KB0TJL
Ryan A Parkin
1720 Ryan Dr
Bismarck ND 58501

WB0HBY
Alvin F Hinkel
Rfd 2 S 12th St
Bismarck ND 58501

KC7QCF
Michelle H Larsen
725 S 12th St Lot 58
Bismarck ND 58504

KF6ZCN
Donna M Abrahamson
1310 S 3rd St
Bismarck ND 58504

KC0UAV
Albert L Reed
509 S 10th St
Bismarck ND 58504

N0XMP
Scott T Williams
612 S 11 St
Bismarck ND 58504

K0ATI
Thomas L Williams
612 S 11th St
Bismarck ND 58501

K0TLW
Thomas L Williams
612 S 11th St

Bismarck ND 58504

WD0EUV
Evalee R Williams
612 S 11th St
Bismarck ND 585045833

KD0QBY
Peter L Petz
725 S 12th St 101
Bismarck ND 58504

N0UXY
Robert R Diede
311 S 14th St
Bismarck ND 58504

KI0QS
Clyde N Zimbelman
506 S 16th St
Bismarck ND 58501

KC0RTP
Nd Division Of Emergency Mgt
Operations Center
712 S 16th St
Bismarck ND 58504

K0HLS
Nd Division Of Emergency Mgt
Operations Center
712 S 16th St
Bismarck ND 58504

KB0CGK
Delores C Tracy
712 S 16th St
Bismarck ND 58504

KB0PWX
Delores C Tracy
712 S 16th St
Bismarck ND 58504

KC0AHL

Hillside Amateur Radio Club
712 S 16th St
Bismarck ND 58504

N0TC
Robert C Tracy
712 S 16th St
Bismarck ND 58504

KC0MXH
Christopher C Tracy
712 S 16th St
Bismarck ND 58504

WA0TOF
Harold H Hoffman
801 S 17 St
Bismarck ND 58504

K0HDA
Raymond L De Boer
602 S 17th
Bismarck ND 58504

KC0RNX
R S T Club
603 S 17th St
Bismarck ND 58504

NO0TA
R S T Club
603 S 17th St
Bismarck ND 58504

WA0RST
Ralph A Spier
603 S 17th St
Bismarck ND 585046141

K0RST
Ralph A Spier
603 S 17th St
Bismarck ND 585046141

N0WRD

Mavis E Hoffman
801 S 17th St
Bismarck ND 58504

Chas L Carlson
6130 SE 12th St
Bismarck ND 58504

KC0NWY
Archie S Goodrich
1316 S 3rd St
Bismarck ND 58504

N0EAO
Patrick J Spilman
6315 Serene Circle
Bismarck ND 58503

KB0PQB
Archie S Goodrich
1316 S 3rd St
Bismarck ND 58504

KA0WMJ
Nicolae C Gheorghe
312 Shady Ln
Bismarck ND 58501

N0JGW
John R Tuthill
1302 S 7th St
Bismarck ND 58504

K0BFD
Jeffrey R Mc Connell
2532 Sharps Loop
Bismarck ND 58503

KB0VNX
June M Tuthill
1302 S 7th St
Bismarck ND 585046537

WB0GFZ
Craig R Schmidt
124 Sioux Ave
Bismarck ND 58501

N0BDR
Monte C Doerr
357 S Brandon Loop
Bismarck ND 58503

KB0MX
Dennis D Julson
6331 Sonora Way
Bismarck ND 58501

N0XMQ
Arthur L Carlson
1224 S Highland Acres Rd
Bismarck ND 58501

N0ONE
Peter R Davidson
921 Southport Loop
Bismarck ND 58504

KB0RLY
Lonnie G Hoffer
1412 S Reno Dr
Bismarck ND 58504

N0TCB
Linda S Davidson
921 Southport Loop
Bismarck ND 58504

KC0ZDQ
Eric S Nagel
4711 Sagebrush Dr
Bismarck ND 58501

WB6CWJ
Arthur C Vorpahl
5406 Southview Ln
Bismarck ND 58501

KC0UAF

KC0FDJ

Leola D Olson
427 Southwood Ave
Bismarck ND 585046258

KC0PAG
Edwin R Ryen
2111 St Joseph Dr
Bismarck ND 58501

KC0PGA
Erik E Ryen
2111 St Joseph Dr
Bismarck ND 58501

N0MBA
Ryan Z Teller
122 Sunrise Ave
Bismarck ND 58501

KC0ZDN
Michael W Jennens
7405 Sunshine Ln
Bismarck ND 58503

KB0RLX
Bobby L Pedigo
9130 Sycamore Ln
Bismarck ND 58504

KA0UAX
Douglas C Kane
132 Telstar Dr
Bismarck ND 58501

N0EPK
Marshall J Murdoch
319 Telstar Dr
Bismarck ND 585030483

N0WJM
Daniel A Polk
1345 Territory Dr
Bismarck ND 585030169

KC0AIV

Jack L Olson
10909 Toulon Drive
Bismarck ND 58503

KD0LWP
David A Rittmiller
4731 Trenton Dr
Bismarck ND 58503

KC0CAU
Randall D Tietz
4512 Turnbow Ln
Bismarck ND 585035816

KD0KPI
John Clemo
2518 Tyler Parkway
Bismarck ND 58503

N0GEE
Ervin J Kuchynski
2707 Tyler Pky
Bismarck ND 585030879

W0BIS
Noaa Operational Amateur Association
2301 University Dr Bldg 27
Bismarck ND 58504

N0ERE
Charles A Swenson Jr
1119 University Dr Lot 1202
Bismarck ND 58504

KC0BXD
Janeen J Swenson
1119 University Dr 1202
Bismarck ND 58504

KC0BXC
Charles A Swenson Jr
1119 University Dr Lot 1202
Bismarck ND 58504

N0PSX

Carl S Erdahl
501 W Ave F
Bismarck ND 58501

N0ZBQ
Arlene R Erdahl
501 W Ave F
Bismarck ND 58501

W0QWG
Donald H Lochner
602 W Ave F
Bismarck ND 58501

KC0MNG
Tony A Zachmeier
609 W Rosser
Bismarck ND 58501

WB0SWY
Andy G Larson
616 W Turnpike Ave
Bismarck ND 58501

K0ZXT
Andrew G Larson
616 W Turnpike Ave
Bismarck ND 58501

KA0LAB
Mark E Peltz
1415 W 15th St
Bismarck ND 58501

KC0EMQ
Richard P Dennis
404 W Apollo Ave 103
Bismarck ND 58503

K0GRM
Dennis R Murphy
111 W Arikara Av
Bismarck ND 585012604

N0WWJ

Christine J Kuchler
200 W Brandon Dr
Bismarck ND 58501

N0YCF
Edward P Kehrwald
200 W Brandon Dr
Bismarck ND 58501

WB0NAD
Raymond J Staiger
423 W Century 207
Bismarck ND 58501

KD0KWU
Robert I Grey Eagle
812 W Divide Ave
Bismarck ND 58501

KC0PDE
David L Graham
305 W Edmonton
Bismarck ND 58503

N0KIF
Chad R Grondahl
462 W Edmonton Dr
Bismarck ND 58501

W0DD
Robert C Luyben
2022 W Harbor Drive
Bismarck ND 585048909

KC0MOJ
Luke R Schafer
4410 W Heart Place
Bismarck ND 58504

W0VAL
Alvin L Anderson
1016 W Highland Acres Rd
Bismarck ND 58501

KC0RKO

Margery P Graham
1025 W Owens
Bismarck ND 58501

KA0KZW
Edgar W Schmidt
110 W Seminole
Bismarck ND 58501

KD0DDR
Gary H Zentz
1016 W Sweet Ave
Bismarck ND 58504

N0XMO
Lynn O Bryntesen
816 W Sweet Ave
Bismarck ND 58504

K0RLD
Raymond L Deboer
903 W Sweet Ave
Bismarck ND 58504

KC0PFW
Bruce C Britton
602 W Thayer Ave
Bismarck ND 58501

KC0PFX
Owen A Britton
602 W Thayer Ave
Bismarck ND 58501

KC0PFY
Delmer W Dyk
1707 W Wichita Dr
Bismarck ND 58504

KC0PFZ
Darren W Dyk
1707 W Wichita Dr
Bismarck ND 58504

KD0KWV

Nathan M Buchholz
5425 Walker Dr
Bismarck ND 58504

KB0QYY
Philip C Miller
1220 Ward Rd
Bismarck ND 585012481

KC0AIU
Gregory K Smith
9100 Wentworth Dr
Bismarck ND 58501

KC0OXX
Delane R Meier
9321 Wentworth Dr
Bismarck ND 585036507

KB0DRM
De Lane R Meier
9321 Wentworth Dr
Bismarck ND 585036507

KC0IW
Duane A Mischel
1101 Westwood St Apt 319
Bismarck ND 58504

KB0VHN
Jason F Steffan
2431 Winchester Dr
Bismarck ND 58503

N0GER
Kallee A Gabel
2141 Xavier St 205
Bismarck ND 58501

WB0VKH
Jodi J Stiles
603 Yorkshire Ln
Bismarck ND 58504

N0IQL

Robert W Ackerman
Bismarck ND 58502

N0DGO
Le Roy C Olson
Bismarck ND 58501

W0MKD
Robert K Watts
Bismarck ND 58502

KA0BUJ
Irene Job
Bismarck ND 58507

W0ZRT
Central Dakota Amateur Rad Club Inc
Bismarck ND 58507

WB0SWV
Howard A Job
Bismarck ND 58507

KC0KVT
Noaa Operational Amateur Association
Bismarck ND 585021016

WB9YMY
Walker A Wynkoop
Bismarck ND 585021372

## FCC Amateur Radio Licenses in Bottineau

W0FPW
Howard M Klingbeil
1050 98th St NE
Bottineau ND 58318

N0HJM
Martha K Straw
1710 99th St NE
Bottineau ND 583186135

WB0NMD

James L Alberta
Box 101
Bottineau ND 58318

WB0NWQ
Jerry R Hegdahl
10451 CR 49
Bottineau ND 58318

KX0Q
George Carbonneau
630 Kersten St
Bottineau ND 58318

KB0TJQ
Timothy L Brosseau
10575 Sjule Rd
Bottineau ND 58318

KC0TYB
Jay L Alberta
Bottineau ND 58318

W0IZA
Merton P B Utgaard
Bottineau ND 58318

## FCC Amateur Radio Licenses in Bowbells

KD0JCD
Bowbells School Amateur Radio Club
200 Madison Ave
Bowbells ND 58721

W0ABQ
Julius J Steffen
Main St
Bowbells ND 58721

N0WZT
Howard R Jacobson
320 Railroad Ave
Bowbells ND 58721

KD0FVE
Cedric Halvorson
Bowbells ND 58721

K7LXT
Lester J Eide
17 2nd Ave NW
Bowman ND 58623

KB0DYA
Duane E Schaff
103 4th Ave SW
Bowman ND 58623

KC0ZPI
Kady E Hansey
106 4th Ave SW
Bowman ND 58623

KC0ZPH
Tyler J Hansey
106 4th Ave SW
Bowman ND 58623

KD0KDY
Kady E Hansey
106 4th Ave SW
Bowman ND 58623

KD0TJH
Tyler J Hansey
106 4th Ave SW
Bowman ND 58623

KC0ROR
Rhonda O Redetzke
106 4th Ave SW
Bowman ND 586230174

N0EHL
Dean A Pearson
20 7th Ave NW Box 589

Bowman ND 58623

KB0DYB
Karey B Schaff
Box 1024
Bowman ND 58623

KB0HYA
Jeremie J Mihulka
Box 1149
Bowman ND 58623

KC0GXG
State Line Amateur Radio Club
Rt 1 Box 51A
Bowman ND 58623

N0LWX
Raymond H Wilkens
Box 702
Bowman ND 58623

KB0PSZ
Terry A Schaefer
Box 776
Bowman ND 58623

KB0EQJ
Brent O Kline
Rt 2 Box 88
Bowman ND 58623

KB0CDX
Le Roy D Van Eckhout
Box 28 Rr 2
Bowman ND 58623

N0QY
Larry W Fischer
602 W Divide
Bowman ND 58623

KC0QOW
South West Ham Operators
1002 W Divide

Bowman ND 58623

ND0UG
South West Ham Operators
1002 W Divide
Bowman ND 58623

KC0UKS
Western Dakota Emergency Operations
Cent
1002 W Divide
Bowman ND 58623

WD0EOC
Western Dakota Emergency Operations
Cent
1002 W Divide
Bowman ND 58623

KC0EAJ
Christopher D Buchholz
1002 W Divide
Bowman ND 58623

N0JAN
Douglas W Buchholz
1002 W Divide
Bowman ND 58623

N0KNE
Laurel J Buchholz
1002 W Divide
Bowman ND 58623

KC0JYK
Matthew A Buchholz
1002 W Divide
Bowman ND 58623

KB0DYA
State Line Amateur Radio Club
1002 W Divide
Bowman ND 58623

KB0IJP

Lori A Steyer
1005 W Railway
Bowman ND 58623

KB0HYU
Heather P Mihulka
Bowman ND 58623

KB0QYO
Nancy A Schaefer
Bowman ND 58623

KB0ZHN
Larry W Fischer
Bowman ND 58623

WB0EYM
Albert L Holecek
Bowman ND 58623

KC0RRR
Rodney R Redetzke
Bowman ND 586230174

## FCC Amateur Radio Licenses in Brinsmade

KC0HGG
Curtis D Lunde
5408 60th Ave NE
Brinsmade ND 583519527

K0UD
Kevin C Lunde
143 Elm St W
Brinsmade ND 583512008

## FCC Amateur Radio Licenses in Buchanan

KB0PEG
Amos J Diede
7055 25 R St SE
Buchanan ND 58420

KC0EON
Richard A Perleberg
7600 28 R St SE
Buchanan ND 58420

## FCC Amateur Radio Licenses in Burlington

KC0AGO
Keith R Reimche
16100 19th Ave NW
Burlington ND 58722

KC0DTR
Sherie M Reimche
16100 19th Ave NW
Burlington ND 58722

WA0CYW
Charles W Johnk
16100 19th Ave NW
Burlington ND 587229538

KB0OXM
Denise M Jost
10 Elm St
Burlington ND 58722

N0IWE
Brian D Jost
10 Elm St
Burlington ND 58722

KC0PQU
David J Rayburn
100 Soo St
Burlington ND 58722

KC0BSP
Dean F Reiter
Burlington ND 58722

## FCC Amateur Radio Licenses in Buxton

KC0NCW
Chris J Schmidt
1495 168th Ave NE
Buxton ND 58218

W0TOM
Lowell A Breiland
Rr 1 Box 145
Buxton ND 58218

KB0WR
Wallace M Domier
Route 1 Box 25
Buxton ND 58218

## FCC Amateur Radio Licenses in Cando

N0TIE
Tiece D Foust
304 4th Ave
Cando ND 58324

KF6BPP
Tiece D Foust
304 4th Ave
Cando ND 58324

KD0NVU
Larry B Halverson
8246 68th Ave NE
Cando ND 58324

KD0NVV
Gary C Rader
7574 72nd Ave NE
Cando ND 58324

KD0NVW
Nancy A Rader
7574 72nd Ave NE
Cando ND 58324

KC0HFW
James L Armey

6769 72nd St NE
Cando ND 58324

W0USY
James L Armey
6769 72nd St NE
Cando ND 58324

KD0NVT
Scott E Walters
720 9th Ave
Cando ND 58324

KB0MCV
Danny R Olson
Rt 1 Box 110
Cando ND 58324

WD0CVQ
Paul E Krack
6925 Hyw 281
Cando ND 583249285

W0JW
George H Hilts
307 Main St 745
Cando ND 583240745

KC0UIS
Jared A Johnson
Cando ND 58324

KG0JO
Robert J Gaffrey
Cando ND 58324

## FCC Amateur Radio Licenses in Carpio

KB0NL
Fred C Johnson
7765 Hwy 28
Carpio ND 58725

KA0QBN

Betty V Johnson
RR 1
Carpio ND 58725

KA0JTL
Darrell L Helseth
Carpio ND 587250003

## FCC Amateur Radio Licenses in Carrington

KB0VHD
Mike R Larson
185 14th Ave N
Carrington ND 58421

KC0DBJ
John T Gallagher
554 1st St S
Carrington ND 58421

KI6NMK
Blaine Hulbert
946 1st St S Apt 5
Carrington ND 58421

KB0GNG
Robert J Mccaffrey
1449 1st St N
Carrington ND 58421

KC0CSN
Ryan E Roaldson
55 1st St N 18
Carrington ND 58421

N0RDJ
Richard D Engel Sr
684 2nd St S
Carrington ND 58421

KI0KC
Harold D Petsinger
72 3rd Ave N
Carrington ND 584211724

KB0VHF
Tim G Hoffman
6260 4th St SE
Carrington ND 584218667

KC0CSM
Dale H Townsend
473 6th Ave S
Carrington ND 584212318

KC0KZJ
Hawksnest Repeater Assn
50 80th Ave SE
Carrington ND 58421

K0ATK
Hawksnest Repeater Assn
50 80th Ave SE
Carrington ND 58421

KR0W
Lynn R Schroeder
50 80th Ave SE
Carrington ND 584218564

K0RGH
Eugene W Edwardson
Rr 1 Box 95
Carrington ND 58421

KA7LRH
Bill D Edwards
215 Cottonwood Ave S
Carrington ND 58421

KA0DPL
Larry P Schroeder
7640 Main St E
Carrington ND 58421

KB0VHE
Tim L Schroeder
7640 Main St E
Carrington ND 58421

KB0ZRL
Scott A Hafner
515 Mc Kenzie Ave
Carrington ND 58421

K0MAD
Marvin L Dunn
807 S 1st
Carrington ND 58421

## FCC Amateur Radio Licenses in Carson

KC7VDX
Theresa Cummins
Carson ND 58529

## FCC Amateur Radio Licenses in Cartwright

KB0FDK
Linda S Chale
Box 87
Cartwright ND 58838

## FCC Amateur Radio Licenses in Casselton

K0GPX
Gerald G Parker
351 12th Ave N
Casselton ND 58012

KB0QAQ
Winfred S Renner Jr
930 Front St 8
Casselton ND 58012

N0OJG
Richard D Kjonaas
361 Langer Ave S  26
Casselton ND 58012

## FCC Amateur Radio Licenses in Cathay

ND0B
William R Ockert
1119 Hwy 30
Cathay ND 58422

WB0VHW
William R Ockert
1119 Hwy 30
Cathay ND 58422

## FCC Amateur Radio Licenses in Cavalier

KC0QAL
Pembina County Amateur Radio Club
Inc
13736 100th St NE
Cavalier ND 58220

N0CAV
Pembina County Amateur Radio Club
Inc
13736 100th St NE
Cavalier ND 58220

WA0YSF
Harold L Mc Connell
13736 100th St NE
Cavalier ND 58220

WA0GWD
Merlyn Dalsted
9713 133rd Ave NE
Cavalier ND 58220

KC0QFL
Megan E Green
13901 95th St NE
Cavalier ND 58220

WA0GWE
John A Dalsted

Rr 1 Box 88
Cavalier ND 58220

KA0PXC
Merton R Beaudrie
13507 CR 1
Cavalier ND 58220

KA0PXD
Judy D Beaudrie
13507 CR 1
Cavalier ND 58220

KC0QFM
Gina B Quinnell
9217 CR 12
Cavalier ND 582209641

N0BUB
James L Cranston
310 E 1st Ave S
Cavalier ND 58220

KB0POJ
Lois J Coggon
307 E 2nd Ave S
Cavalier ND 58220

WB0FBF
Lorraine F Mc Connell
204 E 3rd Ave S
Cavalier ND 58220

KD0MUC
James D Demell
304 Elizabeth St
Cavalier ND 58220

KB0YKD
Donald S Thomson
502 Main St W
Cavalier ND 58220

K0BGV
Earl P Collison

107 Park St E
Cavalier ND 582200190

N0ZMV
Ethel R Collison
107 Park St E
Cavalier ND 582200190

KG6FGL
Gregory S Peterson Mr
706 River St  10
Cavalier ND 58220

KB0TJN
Anna A Maes
98 St NE
Cavalier ND 58220

KD0NMM
Donald S Roberts
Cavalier ND 58220

## FCC Amateur Radio Licenses in Center

N0IYN
Larry J Orgaard
2945 26th St
Center ND 585309563

K0VF
Duane E Hagen
Box 2216
Center ND 58530

KE0VF
Duane E Hagen
Box 2216
Center ND 58530

K7PKV
Jake J Haag
Hc 2 Box 346
Center ND 58530

KB0OFI
Sandra K Letzring
316 Butte Ave S
Center ND 58530

KB0LER
Jeremy D Hagen
130 Interstate St
Center ND 58530

KB0LEQ
Daryl L Hagen
Box 2216 Interstate St
Center ND 58530

KA0SMR
John F Mccauley
122 Klein Ave
Center ND 585300191

KB0PAN
Terry R Wipf
Center ND 58530

N0LWY
Douglas O Letzring
Center ND 58530

## FCC Amateur Radio Licenses in Cleveland

KA0VWQ
Russell P Trautman
6420 35th St SE
Cleveland ND 58424

## FCC Amateur Radio Licenses in Cliffton

WB0RMS
Gary L Youngquist
Rt 1 Box 62
Cliffton ND 58016

## FCC Amateur Radio Licenses in Cogswell

W0RV
Roger D Mallberg
9114 121st Ave SE
Cogswell ND 58017

W0JU
Roger D Mallberg
9114 121st Ave SE
Cogswell ND 58017

## FCC Amateur Radio Licenses in Coleharbor

WD0DXY
Ronald D Gulbranson
3375 14th St NW Lot 33
Coleharbor ND 58531

WB0SWS
Dean W Newton
Rr 1 Box 43 H
Coleharbor ND 585319738

## FCC Amateur Radio Licenses in Colfax

K0RMT
John A Lee
Colfax ND 58018

## FCC Amateur Radio Licenses in Columbus

KD0HXW
Kyle M Hawkins
611 Robin St
Columbus ND 58727

AC0XD
Kyle M Hawkins
611 Robin St

Columbus ND 58727

## FCC Amateur Radio Licenses in Cooperstown

K0LPG
Lester R Zentz
805 13th St NE
Cooperstown ND 58425

KB0CKV
Janaksinh K Ramaiya
Box 250
Cooperstown ND 58425

KA0OFP
Jon L Turner
804 Howard Ave SW
Cooperstown ND 584250328

N0TZX
Kamalesh Ramaiya
1007 Roberts Ave Box 250
Cooperstown ND 58425

## FCC Amateur Radio Licenses in Crary

K0PVG
Kenneth A Larson
9583 48th St NE
Crary ND 583279200

WD0FFQ
Ramsey County Arc
9583 48th St NE
Crary ND 583279200

KC0OFC
Timothy D Legg
204 Kelly Ave
Crary ND 58327

KB0AOU
Myron E Shelton Sr

101 Owen
Crary ND 58327

## FCC Amateur Radio Licenses in Crosby

WB0CMT
Nathan J Loucks
Crosby ND 58730

## FCC Amateur Radio Licenses in Davenport

N0QAD
Allen M Voelker
Rr 1 Box 12A
Davenport ND 58021

## FCC Amateur Radio Licenses in Dawson

K0LI
Richard Neustel
Box 204
Dawson ND 58428

N0KMO
Richard M Mc Kenzie
Dazey ND 58429

## FCC Amateur Radio Licenses in Deering

KE4PVB
Richard A Howe
15 Mobile Home Estates
Deering ND 587314031

KF4IUM
Carolyn E Howe
15 Mobile Home Estates
Deering ND 587314031

N0ZE

Richard A Howe
15 Mobile Home Estates
Deering ND 587314031

## FCC Amateur Radio Licenses in Denhoff

KI0TF
Michael L Piper
201 Steinbrecker Pl
Denhoff ND 58430

KB8KIY
Michael L Piper
201 Steinbrecker Pl
Denhoff ND 58430

## FCC Amateur Radio Licenses in Devils Lake

K0BWZ
Alvin A Plain
650 13th Ave
Devils Lake ND 58301

WD0HON
Ernest S Nagel
1010 1st St
Devils Lake ND 58301

WD0EUY
James D Nagel
1010 1st St
Devils Lake ND 58301

N0RNC
Paulette F Clemenson
8517 48th St NE
Devils Lake ND 58301

NT0V
Dennis M Clemenson
8517 48th St NE
Devils Lake ND 58301

WA0IOB
Harold J Helten
1110 4th Ave
Devils Lake ND 58301

KB0LZM
Robert E Nelson
1208 4th Ave N
Devils Lake ND 58301

WD0CPZ
Gerald L Nelson
7848 51st St NE
Devils Lake ND 58301

KB0OOQ
Mary O Miller
805 5th Ave
Devils Lake ND 58301

KB0ENF
Jay D Heidbreder
1701 5th Ave N 3
Devils Lake ND 58301

KB0ECN
Myron P Loberg
805 5th St
Devils Lake ND 58301

W0YCL
Arnold L Oehlsen
807 6th St
Devils Lake ND 58301

N0VWC
Richard J Schumacher
305 6th St Box 4
Devils Lake ND 58301

KB0MCW
Paul D Cervinski
809 8th St
Devils Lake ND 58301

N0OHU
Larry R Staven
Rt 5 Box 109
Devils Lake ND 58301

KB0MWW
Wade E Sharbond
Rr 1 Box 187B
Devils Lake ND 58301

W0SHZ
Reginald L Connelly
Rr 5 Box 358
Devils Lake ND 58301

WD0CPY
Duane J Rieger
1311 Cherry Pl
Devils Lake ND 58301

KK0CQ
Duane J Rieger
1311 Cherry Place NE
Devils Lake ND 583011809

KA0SLH
Lloyd G Lorenz
601 College Drive
Devils Lake ND 58301

N0CXT
Byron E Logie
7970 CR 1
Devils Lake ND 58301

N0HAI
Garry W Vick
812 Kelly Ave
Devils Lake ND 58301

N0OHR
Terry M Wallace
Southview W 3
Devils Lake ND 58301

N0UWM
Kent S Rohrer
1221 W 3rd Ave
Devils Lake ND 58301

N0OHS
Jim E Hoff
Devils Lake ND 58301

N0OHT
Roger D Bracken
Devils Lake ND 58301

KB0VNE
Mary A Hoff
Devils Lake ND 58301

KC0BAQ
Arlene D Triebold
Devils Lake ND 583010846

KE0FB
Eugene H Triebold
Devils Lake ND 583010846

## FCC Amateur Radio Licenses in Dickinson

KB0NBX
Gordon A Pavlicek
2919 106th Ave SW
Dickinson ND 58601

KC0ADJ
Linda Pavlicek
2919 106th Ave SW
Dickinson ND 58601

KC0PNO
Luke J Schields
3797 10th Ave E
Dickinson ND 58601

N0LVW
Sharon F Gegelmann

3797 10th Ave E
Dickinson ND 58601

WB0OAJ
Mark D Schields
3797 10th Ave E
Dickinson ND 58601

N0UD
Prairie Contesters
3797 10th Ave E
Dickinson ND 586017808

KC0HXF
Rebekah L Schields
3797 10th Ave E
Dickinson ND 58601

KC0ICZ
Prairie Contesters
3797 10th Ave E
Dickinson ND 586017808

KD0BDL
Larry D Skwarok
2441 10th Ave W Apt 6
Dickinson ND 58601

KB0NVT
Betty L Kittelson
261 10th St E
Dickinson ND 58601

WD0DAJ
Stanley E Kittelson
261 10th St E
Dickinson ND 58601

KC0HSR
Curtis L Kittelson
261 10th St E
Dickinson ND 58601

KA0UPH
Ryan R Jilek

3671 114 R Ave SW
Dickinson ND 58601

KB0KIP
Jeremy M Emmerich
970 11th Ave W
Dickinson ND 58601

KC0MRT
Floyd F Hushka
1258 12th St W
Dickinson ND 58601

N0MSJ
Aaron M Wilson
823 13th St E
Dickinson ND 58601

KB0KIQ
Jamie R Privratsky
1119 13th St W
Dickinson ND 58601

KD0LC
Wallace E Beaudoin
921 14th Ave E
Dickinson ND 58601

KB0KFT
Barbara Adams Bleth
1191 15th Ave W
Dickinson ND 58601

KD0DDE
Brittany J Koppinger
1151 16th Ave W
Dickinson ND 58601

KC0HSN
Travis M Booke
981 19th St E
Dickinson ND 58601

K0QR
Rick J Wanner

1512 1st St W
Dickinson ND 58601

KC0APN
Darrel J Heick
829 1st St E
Dickinson ND 58601

KC0NHW
Laurie A Heick
829 1st St E
Dickinson ND 58601

KC0KFR
Cordell R Leidholm
503 1st St SW
Dickinson ND 58601

N0SJE
Joel J Bleth
656 21st St W
Dickinson ND 58601

KC0APO
Graham K Swensen
830 22nd St W
Dickinson ND 58601

KC0JNW
Gerald M Wolberg
10760 26th St SW
Dickinson ND 58601

K0DIK
Gerald M Wolberg
10760 26th St SW
Dickinson ND 58601

KC0FKL
Paula Scheeler
826 28 St W
Dickinson ND 58601

KC0ZFK
David N Williams

529 2nd Av W
Dickinson ND 58601

K0HKY
David N Williams
529 2nd Av W
Dickinson ND 58601

KD0AZY
John M Bjorness Jr
1609 2nd Ave
Dickinson ND 58601

KC0FTE
Austin P Zeller
1410 2nd Ave E
Dickinson ND 58601

N0LZP
Thomas R Nichols
1444 2nd Ave E
Dickinson ND 58601

KD0HCR
Jason P Mahto
829 2nd Ave W
Dickinson ND 58601

KD0KRB
Nathan H Clements
1528 2nd St W
Dickinson ND 58601

W0ZCM
Mark M Tollefson
1536 2nd St W
Dickinson ND 58601

KC0RLF
Michael D Lewton
11121 31P St SW
Dickinson ND 58601

N0LZO
Peter D Roise

6501 33rd St SW
Dickinson ND 58601

KD0AAJ
David A Sheppard
112 3rd Ave E
Dickinson ND 58601

KD0AAK
Melissa M Sheppard
112 3rd Ave E
Dickinson ND 58601

N0CI
David A Sheppard
112 3rd Ave E
Dickinson ND 58601

KE6ZYY
David A Sheppard
112 3rd Ave E
Dickinson ND 58601

KB0YBH
Mike P Callahan
1051 3rd Ave W
Dickinson ND 58601

N0QAU
Joseph P Callahan
1051 3rd Ave W
Dickinson ND 58601

N0QAV
Kim B Callahan
1051 3rd Ave W
Dickinson ND 58601

KC0RRJ
Bernard J Krebs
869 3rd Ave W
Dickinson ND 58601

N0UDG
James M Hastings

719 3rd St W
Dickinson ND 58601

KB0NCA
Paul A Kessel
11365 41st St SW
Dickinson ND 58601

KA0SXP
Edward Schaper
10919 44 1/2 R St SW
Dickinson ND 58601

KB0NVU
Bonnie D Schaper
10919 44 1/2 St SW
Dickinson ND 58601

KC0HSQ
Jon P Fettig
140 4th Ave E
Dickinson ND 58601

KD0DDI
Timothy M Little
918 4th Ave E
Dickinson ND 58601

N0FLY
Donald R Senescall
1190 4th Ave E
Dickinson ND 58601

N0NTD
Steven M Pelling
146 4th St W
Dickinson ND 586014319

KA0SXT
Olav B Eidem
331 5th Ave W
Dickinson ND 58601

KD0HCQ
Robert F Allan

1014 5th Ave W
Dickinson ND 58601

KD0AAI
Reshell R Freeman
32 5th St W
Dickinson ND 58601

KD0DDK
Tyler J Opitz
220 5th St E
Dickinson ND 58601

KB0KIR
Chad E Zubke
68 5th St SW
Dickinson ND 58601

KE7VSK
Michael K Cartmill
960 5th St W
Dickinson ND 58601

AC0PR
Michael K Cartmill
960 5th St W
Dickinson ND 58601

KC0JVJ
Curtis L Freeman
32 5th St W
Dickinson ND 586014323

KC0FKK
Robert S Lewis III
8900 62 Ave SW
Dickinson ND 586018400

KA0VZR
David D Logosz
9211 62nd Ave NE
Dickinson ND 58601

KA0WFX
Catherine G Logosz

9211 62nd Ave NE
Dickinson ND 586018534

KB0OXY
Michael J Schaper
1005 6th St W
Dickinson ND 586014734

N0GSI
Darlene H Bauman
146 7th Ave W
Dickinson ND 58601

N0KUV
Burton M Lahn
239 7th Ave W
Dickinson ND 58601

WV0U
Tom N Bauman
146 7th Ave W
Dickinson ND 58601

KB0NBU
Susan R Haakedahl
657 8th Ave W
Dickinson ND 58601

KD0DDG
Darren C Krebs
522 8th St E
Dickinson ND 58601

KD0DDH
Gerald J Krebs
522 8th St E
Dickinson ND 58601

N0JE
Gerald J Krebs
522 8th St E
Dickinson ND 58601

KC0ADK
Richard M Walton

924 8th St E
Dickinson ND 58601

KA0KJG
Carl R Clark
515 9th Ave E
Dickinson ND 58601

N0JTR
Lawrence A Huschka
260 Allen St
Dickinson ND 58601

WD0DAI
Glenn W Nickel
271 Allen St
Dickinson ND 58601

KC0ADI
Debora J Barros
2241 Bosch Pl
Dickinson ND 58601

K0UB
William W Bosch
2243 Bosch Pl
Dickinson ND 58601

WD0DAW
Irene Bosch
2243 Bosch Pl
Dickinson ND 58601

K0ND
Theodore Roosevelt Amateur Radio
Club
2243 Bosch Place
Dickinson ND 58601

KB0ADU
Dwight E Jacobsen
Rt 4 Box 29H
Dickinson ND 58601

N0JSQ

Dennis J Brueni
Rr 1 Box 81
Dickinson ND 58601

KB0ELT
Kornard E Burkle
219 Carlson St
Dickinson ND 58601

W0IRY
Lawrence A Sanders
861 Cherry Ave
Dickinson ND 58601

KC0HSP
Donny W Ladwig
1637 Dickinson Place Drive
Dickinson ND 58601

N0MEB
Jonathan S Revie
531 Dupont
Dickinson ND 58601

KC0HLK
Naomi M Wehner
531 Dupont
Dickinson ND 58601

KC0EWH
Darryl J Wehner
531 Dupont
Dickinson ND 586014588

KC0OMI
Naomi M Wehner
531 Dupont
Dickinson ND 586014588

KB0GQN
Brian T Revie
531 Dupont St
Dickinson ND 58601

N0LZQ

Steven T Revie
531 Dupont St
Dickinson ND 58601

KC0GJG
Richard J Wehner
724 E 1
Dickinson ND 58601

KC0HKR
Evelyn T Wehner
724 E 1st St
Dickinson ND 586015307

K0POP
Nathan A Sorenson
1434 Empire Rd
Dickinson ND 58601

KB0NCC
Erin R Jilek
962 Franklin St
Dickinson ND 58601

KA0BKV
Norbert J Muggli
841 Green St
Dickinson ND 58601

KD0DDJ
Charles A Olsen
841 Green St
Dickinson ND 58601

K0IAB
Otto P Ficek
11447 Hwy 10
Dickinson ND 586019711

KB0OML
Terrance L Schumacher
162 Kuchenski Dr 4
Dickinson ND 58601

KB0VSE

Arthur A Rabe
3770 Lehigh Rd
Dickinson ND 58601

KB0IXX
Duane F Splichal
833 Park Ave
Dickinson ND 58601

KB0RXG
Connie J Williams
868 Park Ave
Dickinson ND 586013908

ND0ND
Radio North Dakota Ops
905 Park Ave
Dickinson ND 58601

KI0LL
Dean E Williams
868 Park Ave
Dickinson ND 58601

K0NP
Club De Nd
905 Park Ave
Dickinson ND 58601

N0ND
Dean R Summers
905 Park Ave
Dickinson ND 58601

KG0FF
Mitch E Geiszler
40 Patterson Lake
Dickinson ND 58601

KC0SP
Roger L Owen
2137 Prairie Ave
Dickinson ND 58601

KB0LEU

Janelle K Yoder
1776 Prairie Ave Apt 14
Dickinson ND 58601

N7EEE
Randy Jilek
3721 Rivers Edge Drive
Dickinson ND 58601

N0SJ
James A Fahy
1003 Sims St
Dickinson ND 58601

KC0CIB
Sara L Fahy
1003 Sims St
Dickinson ND 58601

W6KCC
Markus A Powell
547 W Villard
Dickinson ND 58601

KB0NXB
Christopher J Lohman
36.5 W Villard
Dickinson ND 58601

KC0LSD
Veronica J Janssen
Dickinson ND 58602

K0RJO
Veronica J Lewis
Dickinson ND 58602

W7IKC
Louis O Tysver
Dickinson ND 586020443

### FCC Amateur Radio Licenses in Drake

N0RUO

Robert E Blumhagen
Rr 1 Box 112
Drake ND 58736

K0DWW
Joseph F Moore
Box 128
Drake ND 58736

KC0JYD
Tom A Marvin
4073 Guthrie Rd
Drake ND 58736

## FCC Amateur Radio Licenses in Drayton

KB0MSP
Doris J Kilichowski
15907 86th St NE
Drayton ND 58225

WA0SDQ
Gene T Lusty
205 E Mill Ave
Drayton ND 582254018

WD0ECR
Luilla A Lusty
205 E Mill Ave
Drayton ND 582254018

KD0FJT
John Schnellbach Jr
202 W Divide Ave
Drayton ND 58225

W0DTN
John Schnellbach Jr
202 W Divide Ave
Drayton ND 58225

KC0DCH
James F Byzewski
Drayton ND 58225

## FCC Amateur Radio Licenses in Driscoll

N0VFD
James L Gear
218 1st St SE
Driscoll ND 58532

N0VFC
Rebecca L Gear
Hc 1 Box 47
Driscoll ND 58532

KB0RLR
Alvin R Fried
Driscoll ND 58532

## FCC Amateur Radio Licenses in Dunseith

W0RRH
Marcel I La Joie
Box 160
Dunseith ND 58329

N0HTY
Floyd A Dion
Dunseith ND 58329

## FCC Amateur Radio Licenses in Edgeley

N0FVX
Barry M Toay
8000 63rd St SE
Edgeley ND 584339749

WA0ZXG
Myron D Seitz
8351 74th St SE
Edgeley ND 584339507

KB0GUL
Jeremy D Johannesen

Box 245
Edgeley ND 58433

KB0GLP
Dennis C Anderson
Box 277
Edgeley ND 58433

KB0GUM
Dean A Johannesen
Edgeley ND 58433

KD0QPA
Scott J Tewksbury
Edgeley ND 58433

## FCC Amateur Radio Licenses in Elgin

KD0KPG
Kendra L Ulrich
6345 64th Ave SW
Elgin ND 58533

WA0WLP
Mark J Worcester
205 Main St S
Elgin ND 58533

## FCC Amateur Radio Licenses in Ellendale

KC5ZCH
Charles J Russell Jr
512 3rd St N
Ellendale ND 58436

KB0GLE
Marsha M Beckius
Rr 1 Box 25
Ellendale ND 58436

KB0GUU
Dennis R Rithmiller
Box 421
Ellendale ND 58436

K9TXJ
Thomas C Davis
400 N 1st St
Ellendale ND 58436

KC0ZZW
Resa L Russell
Ellendale ND 58436

K0UJ
John H Beckius
Ellendale ND 58436

WQ0X
Rodger D Biggs
Ellendale ND 584360781

## FCC Amateur Radio Licenses in Elliot

WD0ABO
Terry K Stroh
1084 Ave S
Elliot ND 580510108

## FCC Amateur Radio Licenses in Emerado

N0WQU
Michael E Rosencrans
1663 Oak St NE
Emerado ND 582289796

## FCC Amateur Radio Licenses in Enderlin

WB0SHF
Mark F Bartle
6145 137th Ave SE
Enderlin ND 58027

## FCC Amateur Radio Licenses in Epping

KB0LMV
Lindsay P Jordan
Epping ND 58843

## FCC Amateur Radio Licenses in Fairfield

KB0GLJ
Ruth H Johnson
Hc 1 Box 52
Fairfield ND 58627

KB0GLK
Larry N Johnson
Hc 1 Box 52
Fairfield ND 58627

## FCC Amateur Radio Licenses in Fargo

KB0KZI
Janson M Steffan
1350 10 St S
Fargo ND 58103

KC0EAK
Brandon M Wehner
1510 10th Ave S
Fargo ND 58103

KC0UHT
Alexander G Pratt
4330 10th Ave SW Apt 214
Fargo ND 58103

KB0TVP
Donald R Ellis
2810 10th St N
Fargo ND 58102

KC0FG
James G Stewart
904 10th St S
Fargo ND 58103

KC0DCD
Christopher D Wilkes
1541 10th St N
Fargo ND 58102

KA0ZFK
Mihai E Skokin
1634 10th St N
Fargo ND 58102

KA0CHX
David L Trautmann
1914 10th St N
Fargo ND 581021858

KC0VCX
Trisha L Dominguez
2301 10th St N
Fargo ND 58102

KD6SPR
James George III
3040 10th St N
Fargo ND 58102

KC0YXA
Stacy J Bjorgaard
3829 10th St N
Fargo ND 581021046

KC0SHP
Jordan Bertsch
3607 10th St S
Fargo ND 58104

KD0FBC
William S Sanger
3614 10th St S
Fargo ND 58104

W0SEO
Thomas T Smith
1731 10th St S
Fargo ND 58102

KD0RLH
Daniel A Stroup IV
1211 11 1/2 St N Apt 10
Fargo ND 58102

N0JIY
Charles K Hohnbaum
1442 11th St N
Fargo ND 58102

KB0QHI
Dean W Blatchford
1412 11th St S
Fargo ND 58103

KC0VKQ
John M Zietz
1145 12th St N
Fargo ND 58102

W0CAQ
Douglas H Classon
2826 12th St S
Fargo ND 58103

KB0QOI
Angela J Klubberud
1533 14 1/2 St S
Fargo ND 58103

KB0QWV
Amy L Klubberud
1533 14 1/2 St S
Fargo ND 58103

KB0VLV
Jeannette E Klubberud
1533 14 1/2 St S
Fargo ND 58103

WB0DCE
Gary W Klubberud
1533 14 1/2 St S
Fargo ND 58103

N0NRS
George C Rohrich Jr
1713 14 1/2 St S
Fargo ND 58103

N0OF
Ronny D Barr
1814 14 1/2 St S
Fargo ND 58103

KB0LXL
Shawn L Kreil
1602 14 St S
Fargo ND 58103

KC0YQS
Leslie A Herbranson
1042 14th St N
Fargo ND 58102

W0LAH
Leslie A Herbranson
1042 14th St N
Fargo ND 58102

KD0GWH
Barbara A Herbranson
1042 14th St N
Fargo ND 58102

K0BAH
Barbara A Herbranson
1042 14th St N
Fargo ND 58102

KC0QXI
George R Clark
1102 14th St S
Fargo ND 58103

N0OKU
Rick A Kreil
1602 14th St S
Fargo ND 58103

WB2PSW
William C Botsford
2525 14th St S Apt 206
Fargo ND 58103

KD0PQH
Joseph M Jovonovich
85 15th Ave N
Fargo ND 58102

KC0HIH
Theodore S Clennon
2526 15th St S Apt 34
Fargo ND 58103

KD0NQY
Varinder Singh
1010 15th St N Apt 2
Fargo ND 58102

KE0GC
Fred A Bagg
2802A 15th St S
Fargo ND 58103

KC0PFQ
Timothy C Lamey
601 15th St S
Fargo ND 58103

KE0MW
Chuck D Skeldum
1341 15th St S
Fargo ND 58103

K0FAB
Fred A Bagg
2802A 15th St S
Fargo ND 58103

KC0LOH
Daniel D Hazer
1521 15th St S
Fargo ND 58103

KB0BLX
Wade V A Wyatt
57 16 1/2 Ave N
Fargo ND 58102

KB0QHJ
Patrick C Curran
1012 16 St N
Fargo ND 58102

KC0ARZ
William O Sullivan
1925 16 St S
Fargo ND 58103

W0BOS
William O Sullivan
1925 16 St S
Fargo ND 58103

KC0DCE
Jonathan W Beich
904 16th St N 8
Fargo ND 58102

KC7QWZ
Seth A Eikomstead
4602 16th Ave SW 303
Fargo ND 58103

N0QAI
Glenn M Wittenberg
44 16th Ave N
Fargo ND 58102

KC0AEI
Nathan R Davis
317 16th Ave N
Fargo ND 58102

KB5LSH
Thomas W Trumpbour
3246 16th Ave S 303
Fargo ND 581034557

KD0RKU
Matthew R Cota
1010 16th St N Apt 7
Fargo ND 58102

KC0WIU
Larry S Anderson
1322 16th St S
Fargo ND 58103

WA0KHL
Cornelius M Hunter
705 17 Ave S
Fargo ND 58103

KD0AOB
Jessica M Slaybaugh
4711 17th Ave SW 106
Fargo ND 58103

W0DBH
Edythe A Beste
3253 17th Ave SW 301
Fargo ND 58103

KC0PFT
Patrick R Hanson
6219 17th St N
Fargo ND 58102

KC0VKS
Tyler A Swartzell
1537 17th St S
Fargo ND 58103

N0NRR
Donald J Jenson
3143C 17th St S
Fargo ND 58103

N0DJJ
Donald J Jenson
3143C 17th St S
Fargo ND 58103

K0ZZZ
Steven Z Craft
2202 17th St S 105
Fargo ND 58103

KD0RLI
Loren K Vanderwerff
3006 18th St S
Fargo ND 58103

KB0RSD
Jason A Huck
5742 18th St S
Fargo ND 58104

KC0LOF
Elizabeth W Bennefeld
801 19 St S
Fargo ND 581032428

N0NHU
Daniel A Rustebakke
1426 19 St S
Fargo ND 58103

KB0GLY
Vaughn A Thorstad
301 19th Ave N
Fargo ND 58102

WB0YVX
Gregory H Wettstein
4206 19th Ave N
Fargo ND 58102

K5JUA
Robert C Perkins
510 19th Ave S
Fargo ND 58103

KC0LOK
Shawn C O'Donnell
318 19th St N
Fargo ND 58102

K0CGY
Allan L Bennefeld
801 19th St S
Fargo ND 58103

KD0PQG
Michael A Miller
3457 19th St S
Fargo ND 58104

KB0BUQ
Harold W Patchin
5618 19th St S
Fargo ND 58104

KD0JVW
Inc. Who Cares Amateur Radio Club
5618 19th St S
Fargo ND 58104

KE0DJ
Jerome F Miller
1710 1st St N
Fargo ND 58102

KD0PYC
Sam J Ewen
630 1st Ave N
Fargo ND 58102

KD0GVY
Chris Serani
1320 1st Ave S
Fargo ND 58103

KD0PYB
Aaron N Aaberg
1109 1st St N
Fargo ND 58102

N0ZQG
Edward L Emerson
1142 1st St N
Fargo ND 58102

KB0MEA
Anita M Dueis
2315 2 Ave S
Fargo ND 58103

N0CFR
Robert M Weigl
221 20th Ave N
Fargo ND 58102

N0VZU
Lloyd A Johnson
2374 20th Ave S
Fargo ND 58103

N7NQF
Goodwin O Larson
314 20th St N
Fargo ND 58102

KD0BVH
Oleg L Rusakov
3010 20th St S
Fargo ND 58103

AC0GZ
Eric M Halvorson
409 21st Ave N
Fargo ND 58102

KB0ZAE
Kaci D Duke
2000 21st Ave S  304
Fargo ND 58103

WW0WR
Jon P Engelhardt
5024 21st Ave SW 201
Fargo ND 58103

WN0Q
Donald Bachmeier
706 21st St S
Fargo ND 581032436

N0NRY
Randall J Huseby
401 23 Ave N
Fargo ND 58102

N0NRW
Mark A Carlson
1801 23rd Ave N 16
Fargo ND 58102

N0SCY
Gary W Kopperud
441 23rd St S
Fargo ND 58103

KC0NSR
Paul A Seifert
2001 23rd St S 205
Fargo ND 58103

KB0BNO
Taha Barwary
718 23rd St S 47
Fargo ND 58103

KF0RI
Orin M Savre
104 2416-26 Ave S
Fargo ND 58103

N0YJY
Daniel J Kerestes
301 24th Ave N
Fargo ND 58102

KB0BQG
Helen D Harris
2208 25 1/2 Ave S
Fargo ND 58103

N0RSS
Rodney S Stoa
2707 25th Ave S
Fargo ND 58103

KC0MOX
Lee A Jorgensen
1608 25th Ave S
Fargo ND 58103

W0BSU
Beaver Bunch University Club Station
1709 25th Ave S 334
Fargo ND 58103

W9NT
Gurnee K Bridgman
1709 25th Ave S Apt 334
Fargo ND 58103

KD0PKS
Timothy P Cruff
2325 26 1/2 Ct S
Fargo ND 58103

K0CRF
Timothy P Cruff
2325 26 1/2 Ct S
Fargo ND 58103

KB0RTW
Robert A Johnson
82 26th Ave N
Fargo ND 58102

KG0IB
Bonnie L Olson
305 27th Ave N
Fargo ND 58102

KD0RLD
Sebastian Patron-Soto
6089 27th St S
Fargo ND 58104

KB0LRN
Pamela C Thompson
1606 28 1/2 Ave S
Fargo ND 58103

N0QAF
Thomas H Thompson
1606 28 1/2 Ave S
Fargo ND 58103

N0ZMW
Pamela C Thompson
1606 28 1/2 Ave S
Fargo ND 58103

WQ0J
Alan D Schoberg
93 28th Ave N
Fargo ND 58102

K0YJY
Donald W Priebe
25 28th Ave NE
Fargo ND 58102

KC0YHO
James A Grettum
3604 28th St S
Fargo ND 58104

N0ZOE
Charles F Lein
1502 29 Ave S
Fargo ND 58103

N0JFP
Jason E Hubert
1906 29th Ave S
Fargo ND 58103

KD0CVZ
Steven D Lee
1530 29th Ave S
Fargo ND 581035921

KC0CCP
Roger A Lessard
708 29th St NW 2
Fargo ND 58102

W0DMJ
Leonard L Riggs
1529 2nd Ave S
Fargo ND 58103

KA7AYO
Pamela E Modin
716 2nd St N
Fargo ND 58102

KC0EXV
Paul R Nelson
1205 2nd St N
Fargo ND 58102

N0CL
Aaron Sprenger
1625 2nd St N
Fargo ND 58102

N0SRN
Karin M Ellingson
3530 2nd St N 22
Fargo ND 58102

AA0RD
Peter D Johnson
3510 2nd St N 9
Fargo ND 58102

KB0JCP
Yoongyong Kim
3522 2nd St N Apt 15
Fargo ND 58102

WB0VBC
Clayton M Hokanson
1522 3 St N
Fargo ND 58102

N0HCI
John T Ortberg
217 30th Ave N
Fargo ND 58102

KB0IXL
Kurt D Lindquist
221 30th Ave N
Fargo ND 58102

KD0RKS
John G Englund III
4279 31st Ave S
Fargo ND 58104

KC0FWJ
Todd E Sheppard
111 32nd Ave N
Fargo ND 58102

N0CFT
Gordon E Severson
815 32nd Ave N 202
Fargo ND 58102

KF0ZK
Sharon M Altendorf
1101 32nd Ave S
Fargo ND 58103

KB0GLV
Steven H Carbno
2111 32nd Ave S
Fargo ND 58103

KC0JCT
Steven H Carbno
2111 32nd Ave S
Fargo ND 58103

KA9RSK
Charles M Krueger
916 32nd St NW
Fargo ND 58102

KC0TAL
Jerry W Reynolds
2822 32nd St SW
Fargo ND 58103

KC0DIS
Richard A Larson
4221 33rd Ave S
Fargo ND 58104

KD0SWM
Scott W Moore
4281 33rd Ave S Apt 204
Fargo ND 58104

K0SWM
Scott W Moore
4281 33rd Ave S Apt 204
Fargo ND 58104

KC0PFO
Naveed A Syed
4201 33rd Ave SW Apt 106
Fargo ND 58104

KC0GVQ
David T Barnick
3049 33rd St S Unit 6
Fargo ND 581037885

KA0KZX
John G Struchynski
2806 33rd St SW
Fargo ND 58103

KC0KCT
Robert K Mynheir
2914 33rd St SW
Fargo ND 58103

KF0TB
Elwyn C Hanson
1603 34 1/2 Ave S
Fargo ND 58104

KC0MPC
Gregory E Mcdonald
2718 34th Ave SW
Fargo ND 58104

KB0SIG
Jamie A Sesti
1429 34th St S
Fargo ND 581036320

AA0CX
Mark A Swartzell
1517 34th St SW Apt 104
Fargo ND 58103

KC0AZV
Daniel C Polk
1430 34th St SW Apt 306
Fargo ND 58103

KC0OGZ
Daniel E Dietz
3201 35 1/2 Court Ave S
Fargo ND 581048879

WB0ROM
Kirk P Jensen
32 35th Ave NE
Fargo ND 58102

KC0TLP
Eric R Jacobson
2202 35th Ave S
Fargo ND 58104

WA0GMQ
Al D Johnson
3242 35th Ave S
Fargo ND 58104

KC0YCO
Jason E Hubert
1601 36 1/2 Ave S
Fargo ND 58104

N0JFP
Jason E Hubert
1601 36 1/2 Ave S
Fargo ND 58104

N9XFX
Dennis P Joiner
2644 36th Ave S Apt 304
Fargo ND 58104

KC0HES
Michael R Erickson
3010 36th St S Unit 9
Fargo ND 581036291

KG5CS
Diane R Nelson
1809 37th Ave S
Fargo ND 58104

KB0KNV
Katie T Yokom
1620 38 1/2 Ave S
Fargo ND 58104

W0TOR
Eric R Whitehill
4285 39 1/2 Ave SW
Fargo ND 58104

KC0MGL
Marilyn Beaton
4277 39th Ave S
Fargo ND 58104

KC0FWG
Joseph P Allen
1342 3rd Ave S
Fargo ND 58103

KC0IVO
Steven A Donaldson
612 3rd St N
Fargo ND 58102

N0STM
Arthur R Streed
1024 3rd St N
Fargo ND 58102

KC0FWH
David P Mrozla
1110 3rd St N
Fargo ND 58102

WB0VBB
Donna J Hokanson
1522 3rd St N
Fargo ND 58102

KD0PYA
William J Kuehn
7105 40th Ave N
Fargo ND 58102

KC9TYN
Sekar Raju
5050 40th Ave S Apt 208
Fargo ND 58104

K3RAJ
Sekar Raju
5050 40th Ave S Apt 208
Fargo ND 58104

KE6ASA
Gary J Olson
3240 40th Ave SW Unit A
Fargo ND 58104

KC0PFL
Bhashwat Risal
1717 40th St S 102
Fargo ND 58103

K0HLT
Walter T Pfeifer
555 40th St SW 125
Fargo ND 58103

WB0OTF
Maxine L Pfeifer
555 40th St SW 125
Fargo ND 58103

KA0QIE
Jonathan W Hinkel
1717 40th St SW 136
Fargo ND 58103

KC0SRY
Tanner K Seibel
1717 40th St SW 338
Fargo ND 58103

KB0SMQ
Phillip J Lohman
1830 42nd St SW Apt 104
Fargo ND 581037150

KD0CRG
Jon C Abel
3700 42nd St S 302
Fargo ND 58104

N0VGV
Michael J Woytassek
3350 42nd St SW 302
Fargo ND 58104

KC0KRQ
Ned A Kautzman
3340 42nd St SW 308
Fargo ND 58104

N0WRC
Darren J Boehm
901 42nd St SW 113
Fargo ND 58103

N0WQX
Kelly G Flynn
566 42nd St SW 365
Fargo ND 58103

KC0PFN
John R Sansburn
903 43rd St SW 205
Fargo ND 58103

KC0YGI
Shannon M Martinson
5001 44th Ave S Apt 309
Fargo ND 58104

KA0PVN
Kent A Heneman
3310 44th Ave S W
Fargo ND 58104

WB0QHC
Gary D Woodbury
4378 44th St S
Fargo ND 58104

N0SCW
Mildred M Tareski
3348 45 St NW
Fargo ND 58102

K0QYW
Val G Tareski
3348 45th St N
Fargo ND 581025400

W0RRW
Ernie Anderson Memorial Station
3348 45th St NW
Fargo ND 58102

KA0ZKP
Lyle J Myrvik Mr.
3447 46th Ave S
Fargo ND 58104

KB0TFH
Andrew R Haug
4397 46th Ave SW
Fargo ND 58104

KD0PXY
Jacob M Parrow
4209 47th St N
Fargo ND 58102

KD0NQX
James A Parrow
4209 47th St N
Fargo ND 58102

KD0IOE
Andrew R Lynch
2036 49th St S 3
Fargo ND 58103

W0OAB
Frances J Evans
1416 4th Ave N
Fargo ND 58102

K0ORQ
Lloyd R Schrade
1008A 4th Ave S
Fargo ND 58103

WB0JOS
Steven R Kereluk Sr
1415 4th Ave S
Fargo ND 58102

KB0FEK
Michael J Schelske
1534 4th Ave S
Fargo ND 58103

W0WXS
Lloyd C Erickson
1113 4th St N
Fargo ND 581023705

KD0RKP
Thomas P Christensen
1325 4th St N
Fargo ND 58102

KD0RKQ
John Christensen
1325 4th St N
Fargo ND 58102

KA0ZOO
Patty D Reed
1530 4th St N
Fargo ND 58102

N0FPL
Leon H Gelinske
1721 4th St N
Fargo ND 58102

KB0QHG
Mark A Norquist
1518 5 Ave N
Fargo ND 58102

WB0QOG
Thomas S Berseth
1909 5 St S
Fargo ND 58103

KD0BVE
Cody A Wangen
1942 55th Ave S
Fargo ND 58104

KA0WTW
Patrick B Phillips
1015 5th Ave S
Fargo ND 58103

KB0KML
Christine A Phillips
1015 5th Ave S
Fargo ND 58103

NK0A
Gerald R Phillips
1015 5th Ave S
Fargo ND 58103

KE0OP
John A Lynn
1324 5th St N
Fargo ND 58103

KD0NRA
Nicholas R Aasand
1608 62nd Ave N
Fargo ND 58102

KD0NRB
Braden C Aasand
1608 62nd Ave N
Fargo ND 58102

N0KMS
Barbara J Pagel
1538 6th Ave S
Fargo ND 58103

N0KCN
J Erin Rourke
1538 6th Ave S
Fargo ND 581032522

W0HKM
John R Konen
1810 6th Ave S
Fargo ND 58102

WB0DQA
Steven J Sprenger
10412 6th St S
Fargo ND 58104

W0WIA
Earl R Orvedal
4301 76th Ave S
Fargo ND 58104

KC0WIV
Paul J Klapperich
202 7th Ave N Apt 5
Fargo ND 58102

N0GUN
Delano C Grimestad
1809 7th Ave S
Fargo ND 58103

KD0HPD
Rodney A Vanbruggen
720 7th N
Fargo ND 58102

KE6LSS
Freeman P Pascal IV
1133 7th St N
Fargo ND 58102

WD0DVM
Micheal C Maassel
2310 7th St N
Fargo ND 58102

KC0MOY
Lester H Hazlett
1701 7th St S
Fargo ND 58103

KB0ZTF
Chris M Sanger
1006 7th St S
Fargo ND 58103

AA0QK
Richard N Johnson
2301 7th St N
Fargo ND 58102

W0RNJ
Richard N Johnson
2301 7th St N
Fargo ND 58102

WB0QPO
Alan L Christopherson
3006 7th St N
Fargo ND 58102

KC0CQJ
Ryan L Haug
2814 7th St N 24
Fargo ND 58012

N0XHH
Perry S Clark
1321 7th St S
Fargo ND 58103

N0QAE
Tom H Novak
1702 7th St S
Fargo ND 58103

N0UWO
Seth T Novak
1702 7th St S
Fargo ND 58103

KC0VKT
Ravindra Deshmukh
315 7th St S Park Terrace 12
Fargo ND 58103

KC0VKU
Jyoti Deshmukh
315 7th St S Park Terrace 12
Fargo ND 58103

WA0JXI
Le Roy A Hinz
4726 8th Ave SW
Fargo ND 581037209

KD0RLE
Matthew S Evans
803 8th St S
Fargo ND 58103

KB0VAQ
Michael D Agee
516 8th St S Apt 8
Fargo ND 58103

KC0VOP
Dennis A Volker
1545 8th St N
Fargo ND 58102

KD0JYZ
Karen J Kohoutek
211 8th St S
Fargo ND 58103

KD0JDJ
Stephen J Baird
1450 8th St S
Fargo ND 58103

W0NYC
Paul R Abrahamson
1614 8th St S
Fargo ND 58103

W0SGF
Paul R Abrahamson
1614 8th St S
Fargo ND 58103

KD0KTN
Michael Ragan
4259 9th Ave Cir S Apt 112
Fargo ND 58103

KC0PFU
Jack L Smith
4226 9th Ave Cir SW Apt 111
Fargo ND 58103

KD0MMN
Bjorn Altenburg
709 9th Ave N
Fargo ND 58102

KC0TEL
David M Muir
1537 9th Ave S
Fargo ND 58103

KD0HPE
Brad J Baltrusch
2210 9th Ave S
Fargo ND 58103

KF0DD
Raymond L Hubbard
1910 9th St N
Fargo ND 58102

KA0LXH
Seymour A Olson
1361 9th St N
Fargo ND 58102

AB0BL
David A Rogers
1502 9th St N
Fargo ND 581022208

N0QAG
Robert C Nordland
1626 9th St N
Fargo ND 58102

WC0G
Peter Pugliano
920 9th St S
Fargo ND 58103

KB0NDH
Scot A Taylor
13 A Ct
Fargo ND 58102

W0GII
Bernard J Des Roches
4563 Adams Dr
Fargo ND 581025415

KC0WXI
Eric M Halvorson
5050 Amber Valley Pkwy -305
Fargo ND 58104

KC0MPA
Drew A Hewitt
208 B
Fargo ND 581055438

K0PVV
Donald A Short
3 Birch Ln
Fargo ND 58103

WB0PGY
Thomas L Elliott
1 Birch Ln
Fargo ND 58103

KB1VSM
Stephen T Kostecke III
5504 Bishops Blvd S Unit C
Fargo ND 581047646

K0STK
Stephen T Kostecke III
5504 Bishops Blvd S Unit C
Fargo ND 581047646

W0EFP
Robert A Harms
Box 1325
Fargo ND 58107

KB0DRM
Robert L Tassin
Rr 1 Box 397
Fargo ND 58103

W0FZJ
Sylvester T Novak
1429 Broadway
Fargo ND 58102

N0WTD
Rex G Lusty
1617 Broadway
Fargo ND 58107

K0ZWG
James B Mowery
2525 Broadway Apt 1006
Fargo ND 58102

KD0NZU
Gerardo Zamora
234 Churchill
Fargo ND 58102

KB0GLV
Steven H Carbno
205 Circle Dr
Fargo ND 58102

KC0VKP
William G Baugh
249 Circle Dr N
Fargo ND 58102

KD0RLJ
Christopher L Runge
1105 College St N Apt Upst
Fargo ND 58102

WB9OII
James E Ziemann
1315 Cossette
Fargo ND 58104

KI0LT
Bradley E Hemerick Mr
4249 Coventry Dr S
Fargo ND 58104

K0JWK
Stuart J Uggen
3126 Dakota Park Cir S
Fargo ND 58104

W0PEW
Raymond T Myers
2501 E Country Club Dr
Fargo ND 58103

KC0VKV
Qun Li
223 E University Village
Fargo ND 58102

KF0XK
Kyongsok Kim
255 E University Village
Fargo ND 58102

KB0ONI
Carol J Carlisle
2923 Edgemont St
Fargo ND 58102

KF0CG
Mark S Carlisle
2923 Edgemont St
Fargo ND 58102

KB0IXN
Angela M Boser
3001 Edgewood Dr
Fargo ND 58102

KB0NVS
William N Gregg
1307 Elm St
Fargo ND 58102

KE0VN
Mark J Ehlen
3202 Elm St
Fargo ND 58102

KA0MMP
Virginia A Gregg
1307 Elm St N
Fargo ND 58102

N0PTP
Lynn E Ehlen
3202 Elm St N
Fargo ND 58102

KB0PDR
Rachel S Fugleberg
2505 Evergreen Rd
Fargo ND 58102

KG0VC
James N Fugleberg
2505 Evergreen Rd
Fargo ND 58102

KC0DCF
Donald S Galitz
2843 Evergreen Rd
Fargo ND 58102

KD0HPF
Michael C O'Keefe
3261 Evergreen Rd
Fargo ND 58102

AA0WV
Jeremy J Fugleberg
2505 Evergreen Rd NE
Fargo ND 58102

KB0M
Carl G Fischer
3708 Fairway Rd
Fargo ND 58102

WB0VKG
Vernon R Kepler
412 Forest River Dr
Fargo ND 58104

KC8GXD
Howard R Etson
1200 Hardwood Dr Apt166
Fargo ND 58104

W0KZZ
Carl W Reed
1200 Harwood Dr 124
Fargo ND 58104

KE0UW
Joel P Jahraus
3037 Hickory St
Fargo ND 58102

KB0MEB
Daron P Desplazes
31 Horseshoe Bend
Fargo ND 58104

KB0NVQ
Douglas E Corbett
19 Horseshoe Trlr Ct
Fargo ND 58104

KD0CWE
David J Mohn
829 Kennedy Ct N
Fargo ND 58102

KB0VSS
Roger G Johnson
2843 Longfellow Rd
Fargo ND 58102

KB0VST
June M Johnson
2843 Longfellow Rd
Fargo ND 58102

N0WRA
Diane M Urich
3018 Madison Ave N
Fargo ND 58102

N0TSZ
James E Kruft
1220 Monte Carlo Dr
Fargo ND 58102

KC0GQE
Lori A Kruft Ms
1220 Monte Carlo Dr
Fargo ND 58102

KC0HIG
Marva J Kruft Mrs
1220 Monte Carlo Dr
Fargo ND 58102

WD0EWM
Julia M Christiansen
314 N 25th Ave
Fargo ND 58102

W0CZ
Kenneth A Christiansen
314 N 25th Ave
Fargo ND 58102

WB0RMR
James W Underwood
2005 N 8th St
Fargo ND 58102

K0ALL
Ronald L Roche
1437 N University Dr
Fargo ND 58102

N0CAT
Milfred T Bakke
308 N 10th St
Fargo ND 58102

KD0ACB
Lew D Dailey
1013 N 16 St
Fargo ND 58107

KI0E
Michael D Olson
305 N 27th Ave
Fargo ND 58102

N0HHG
Robert M Nelson
1205 N 2nd St
Fargo ND 58102

W0WCP
Doris A Wehr
3510 N 2nd St 26
Fargo ND 58102

W0DYA
Robert E Jones
1253 N 5th St
Fargo ND 58102

KD0DOK
Rachel M Jensen
820 N Univ Dr
Fargo ND 58102

KD0EEG
Jason M Beck
1311 N University Dr 2
Fargo ND 58102

KD0CWB
Wayne R Monk
820 N University Drive
Fargo ND 58102

AC0KH
Ryan J Cofell
NDSU 110B Llc
Fargo ND 58105

W0HSC
North Dakota State Univ Ama Rad
Society
NDSU Dept-2480
Fargo ND 58108

KC0GQF
Gerardo Miramontes De Leon
NDSU Dept-2480
Fargo ND 58108

N0NRD
Cornel H Lunzman
2702 Northwood Dr
Fargo ND 58102

WB0RCX
John Korol
127 Oak Manor Ct
Fargo ND 58103

K0VWG
Roger L Laskey
1306 Oak St
Fargo ND 58102

K0PAO
William P Nerhus
702 Oak St N Apt F
Fargo ND 58102

W0OS
James A Grettum
801 Orchard Park Dr
Fargo ND 58104

KC0MPB
Paul J Gregg
3219 Par St N
Fargo ND 58102

AA0NT
Linda L Johnson
3219 Par St NE
Fargo ND 58102

WB0PBQ
Ted C Thode Jr
1701 Park Blvd
Fargo ND 58103

N0UKW
Nathan R Huff
1825 Park Blvd
Fargo ND 58103

KB0VSW
Russell D Trout
383 Prairiewood Cir 203
Fargo ND 58103

KB0QHL
Julian J Mrozla
49 Prairiewood Crossing SW
Fargo ND 58103

N0KQE  
David A Gruhot Jr  
113 Prairiewood Dr  
Fargo ND 58103  

KB0KZJ  
Stacey A Westberg  
279 Prairiewood Dr  
Fargo ND 58103  

N0GJO  
James D Mc Laughlin  
176 Prairiewood Dr SW  
Fargo ND 58103  

KD0GWD  
Jayson F Clairmont  
188 Prariewood Dr  
Fargo ND 58103  

KB0RTU  
Greg G Sickler  
137 Prariewood Dr 305D  
Fargo ND 58103  

KA0CWL  
Jon L Wanzek  
3420 River Dr  
Fargo ND 58104  

KA0WTX  
Mark O Jensen  
4584 Riverwood Drive N  
Fargo ND 58102  

KD0RLF  
Alexander Manz  
5033 Rose Creek Parkway  
Fargo ND 58104  

KC4CDT  
Richard T Budge II  
1629 Round Hill Dr  
Fargo ND 58104  

KB0CW  
George A Dodds  
1602 S 10th St  
Fargo ND 58102  

KF0A  
Bruce L Dahl  
1013 S Dr  
Fargo ND 58103  

N0PTQ  
Barry L Dresser Mr.  
2849 S Gate Drive  
Fargo ND 58103  

KC0OES  
Lee C Spiesman  
401 S University  
Fargo ND 58103  

KC0QZE  
John T Sanger  
3614 S 10th St  
Fargo ND 58104  

KC0ZDC  
John T Sanger  
3614 S 10th St  
Fargo ND 58104  

KA0MWI  
Allen K Tommeraus  
2930 S 11th St  
Fargo ND 58103  

W0LHS  
William D Snyder  
1514 S 12th St  
Fargo ND 58103  

KD0RKO  
Allan L Hagemeier  
1806 S 16th St  
Fargo ND 58103

WB0VCS
Donald E Hedlund
910 S 18th St
Fargo ND 58103

W9MQV
Stuart J Uggen
1010 S 18th St
Fargo ND 58103

N0RZG
Merle D Anderson
1432 S 18th St
Fargo ND 58103

N0SYB
Theresa A Anderson
1432 S 18th St
Fargo ND 58103

W0QCP
Glenn A Paulson
2308 S 18th St D
Fargo ND 58103

WD0EGC
Robert J Goos
1710 S 6 St
Fargo ND 58103

WB0YFU
Jeffrey C Schlossman
1747 S 7th St
Fargo ND 58103

KC0AEK
Gerald M Kuehn
420 S 8th St 16
Fargo ND 58103

N0WTF
Allan D Landers
723 S Eighth St
Fargo ND 58103

KB4WTI
Kevin D Flanagan
3302 S River Dr
Fargo ND 581046262

KC0QXG
Timothy T Erickson
722 S Sedona Place
Fargo ND 58104

KA0LHN
Fred P Anderson
7507 S University Dr
Fargo ND 58104

N0OTH
Connie L Burckhardt
4732 San Juan Dr
Fargo ND 58103

KB0KYN
Steven T Hanson
806 Southwood Dr
Fargo ND 58103

KC0TEM
Andrew J Roberts
215 Stockbridge Ndsu
Fargo ND 58105

KD0CWD
Megan S Bouret
820 Unversity Dr N
Fargo ND 58102

KC0SHM
Mark A Johnson
2849 W Gate Drive
Fargo ND 58103

KC0LOG
Kathy M Hazer
1620 W Gateway Cir S
Fargo ND 58103

KG0FS
Gary P Skramstad
2450 W Country Club Dr
Fargo ND 581035739

W7WXR
Michael E Zavaleta
602 Waco Ln
Fargo ND 58103

N0AML
Alfred M Loktu
3430 Waterford Drive
Fargo ND 58104

NG0I
Alfred M Loktu
3430 Waterford Drive
Fargo ND 58104

KB0BLW
Jayne A Rose
1112 Westrac 304
Fargo ND 58103

KD0LOI
Brad A Olson
2933 Wheatland Dr
Fargo ND 58103

KA0WYG
Kenneth R Johnson
Fargo ND 58107

KD0PQI
Gabe V Thomas
Fargo ND 58106

KB0VHM
Robert E Ruud
Fargo ND 58106

KD0CWC
Ef Dump

Fargo ND 58107

W0BSL
Richard D Overby
Fargo ND 58107

W0ILO
Red River Radio Amateurs
Fargo ND 58108

WB7VZZ
George E Brumm Jr
Fargo ND 581082394

KC0KAE
Red River Radio Amateurs
Fargo ND 581083215

FCC Amateur Radio Licenses in
Fessenden

WD0DFT
Ronald L Lamm
1233 44th Ave NE
Fessenden ND 58438

KC0EEY
Ermalene A Baltrusch
Box 373
Fessenden ND 58438

KB2TZE
Bruce R La Plant
719 Court St
Fessenden ND 58438

WB6HEF
Curtis L Delzer
218 Harriet Ave
Fessenden ND 584387300

KI0NS
Lynn A Baltrusch
314 Hope Ave NE
Fessenden ND 584380373

## FCC Amateur Radio Licenses in Fingal

KB0QYU
Norma N Duppler
4605 CR 21
Fingal ND 58031

## FCC Amateur Radio Licenses in Finley

WA0RWI
Donald J Huso
12824 8th St NE
Finley ND 58230

KA0PLK
Mason M Linnell
313 N Lincoln
Finley ND 582300026

WD0HBU
James F Martin
205 W 3rd St
Finley ND 58230

KA0PDV
Delphine K Martin
Finley ND 582300545

## FCC Amateur Radio Licenses in Flasher

N0MBF
Arlys A Krause
Rr 1 Box 68
Flasher ND 58535

N0TFE
Jackie M Krause
Rt 1 Box 68
Flasher ND 58535

KA0SML

Delbert D Krause
RR 1
Flasher ND 58535

KA0SPS
Kirby L Krause
RR 1
Flasher ND 58535

## FCC Amateur Radio Licenses in Flaxton

K0HJ
Harold W Jacobson
Rr 2 Box 53A
Flaxton ND 58737

KA0NRT
Marie E Jacobson
Rr 2 Box 53A
Flaxton ND 58737

## FCC Amateur Radio Licenses in Fordville

KC0NCX
Warren J Wambsganss
4750 33rd Ave NE
Fordville ND 58231

## FCC Amateur Radio Licenses in Forman

KA0WVO
Kurt J Kosmatka
Box 36
Forman ND 58032

KB0QZG
Sandra A Hanson
12787 Hwy 11
Forman ND 580329798

## FCC Amateur Radio Licenses in Fort Ransom

N0ZLN
David H Carlson
Rr 1 Box 51
Fort Ransom ND 58033

KB0VSR
Lori L Carlson
155 Mill Rd
Fort Ransom ND 58033

## FCC Amateur Radio Licenses in Fort Yates

KA5QIQ
Pat L Phillips
Fort Yates ND 58538

## FCC Amateur Radio Licenses in Fredonia

KB0YOR
Todd T Wilen
6664 59th Ave SE
Fredonia ND 584409776

## FCC Amateur Radio Licenses in Gardner

KE7FAO
Clinton A Wethered
201 2nd Ave W
Gackle ND 58442

KD0GWF
Bradley D Larson
1908 163rd Ave SE
Gardner ND 58036

## FCC Amateur Radio Licenses in Garrison

N0MGL
John M Iglehart
5635 15th St NW
Garrison ND 585409392

W0HNW
Leland W Jones
119 4th St SE
Garrison ND 58540

KB0STL
Dustin J Kovarik
1706 56th Ave NW
Garrison ND 58540

## FCC Amateur Radio Licenses in Gilby

KC0PDA
David W Soderman
3305 28th Ave NE
Gilby ND 58235

## FCC Amateur Radio Licenses in Gladstone

KB0RXI
George F Grassel Jr
4245 99th Ave SW
Gladstone ND 58630

KB0IZZ
Gordon H Muecke
Hco 1 Box 15
Gladstone ND 58630

KB7ITR
Margaret M Wieglenda
Box 306
Gladstone ND 58630

N0DK
Emil F Wieglenda
Box 306
Gladstone ND 58630

N0YSY
Allen J Sickler
Hc1 Box 36
Gladstone ND 58630

K7TNY
Anthony R Aman
217 Cliff St
Gladstone ND 58630

KA7LQB
Marjorie A Aman
Gladstone ND 58630

KB0RXJ
Marvin A Cassezza
Gladstone ND 58630

KC0HKS
Anthony R Aman
Gladstone ND 58630

## FCC Amateur Radio Licenses in Glen Ullin

N1ULC
Joseph M Fink
5801 41st St
Glen Ullin ND 58631

KD0DDD
Dennis D Hintz
3975 68th Ave E Box 667
Glen Ullin ND 58631

K0HL
Kenneth L Muggli
306 Main St S
Glen Ullin ND 58631

N7IYZ
Kenneth L Muggli
306 Main St S
Glen Ullin ND 58631

KD7RDD
Jerome A Zimmerman
111 S B St
Glen Ullin ND 58631

W0ZTL
Alexander J Muggli
405 S D St
Glen Ullin ND 586310713

KD7QDN
Kari R Zimmerman
111 S B St
Glen Ullin ND 58631

## FCC Amateur Radio Licenses in Glenburn

KD0JNK
Christopher E Whited
2740 76th St NW
Glenburn ND 58740

KC0KNP
Lyle E Freeman
2775 76th St NW
Glenburn ND 587409715

KC0VEQ
Gregory W Swenson
Glenburn ND 58740

KB0PUQ
Gregory W Swenson
Glenburn ND 58740

## FCC Amateur Radio Licenses in Glenfield

WA0FXO
David L Utke
140 92nd Ave NE
Glenfield ND 584439376

## FCC Amateur Radio Licenses in Goodrich

N0YPD
Michael S Gesellchen
204 1st St E
Goodrich ND 58444

## FCC Amateur Radio Licenses in Grafton

WD0EEP
Fred Goldstone
6645 154 Ave NE
Grafton ND 58237

K0MDB
Raymond W Schultz
660 Birch Ct
Grafton ND 58237

N0KHM
Renee A Keller
840 Cooper Ave
Grafton ND 58237

W0VKB
Earl R Durheim
600 E 9th St
Grafton ND 58237

KA0ERF
Terrence J Conlon Sr
816 Griggs Ave
Grafton ND 58237

WB0BPD
George J Kovash
1434 Lawler Ave
Grafton ND 58237

KB0ERR
James O Renslow
1444 Lawler Ave
Grafton ND 58237

KB0CH
Melvin F Malafa
1451 Lawler Ave
Grafton ND 58237

WA0ZYY
William O Field
335 W 6th St
Grafton ND 582371370

## FCC Amateur Radio Licenses in Grand Forks

N0RNF
Michael J Derman
1730 10th Ave N
Grand Forks ND 58203

KB0MGU
William J Meenk
2014 11 Ave N
Grand Forks ND 58203

W7LZZ
William J Meenk
2014 11 Ave N
Grand Forks ND 58203

KB0JZT
Terry K Merriman
3514 11 Ave N 14
Grand Forks ND 58203

KD0RLG
Raymond D Mills
3533 11th Ave N
Grand Forks ND 58203

KB0DBM
Colby A Lysne
3615 11th Ave N
Grand Forks ND 58201

KC0UBI

Michelle L Stele
3538 11th Ave N Apt 23
Grand Forks ND 58203

N7BDO
Richard J Bennett
1602 13th Ave S
Grand Forks ND 58201

KA0HHJ
Bobby L Vogel
2500 14th Ave S Apt 11
Grand Forks ND 58201

NX0K
John S Lynch
624 19th Ave S
Grand Forks ND 58201

KA0ZEN
Isis E Lynch
624 19th Ave S
Grand Forks ND 582017336

KB0YFK
Jeffrey J Ramsey
1119 19th Ave S
Grand Forks ND 58201

KA0CAF
Paul S Slusar
1816 1st Ave N
Grand Forks ND 58201

WA0JXT
Forx Amateur Radio Club Inc
1816 1st Ave N
Grand Forks ND 58201

N0YJZ
Paul H Olson
2010 1st Ave N
Grand Forks ND 58203

KC0RJD

Ryan J Schmidt
2026 1st Ave N
Grand Forks ND 58203

N0MUE
Mark W Rogers
3415 20th Ave S 422
Grand Forks ND 58201

KC0FTG
Scott G Tolbert
1010 22nd Ave S
Grand Forks ND 58201

KD0OSK
Cameron L Ericson
3774 22nd Ave S
Grand Forks ND 58201

KC0ODE
Seth J Swenson
2828 B 22nd Ave S
Grand Forks ND 58201

KG6EIL
Kenneth R Medd
1203 22nd St S
Grand Forks ND 58201

KC0GWK
Jerry L Moran
605 24th Ave S
Grand Forks ND 58201

K0VOO
Roger E Syvertsen
611 25th Ave S
Grand Forks ND 58201

N8UCY
Florence J Syvertsen
611 25th Ave S
Grand Forks ND 58201

KB0YKE

Richard C Bjornstad
2701 26th St S Apt 16
Grand Forks ND 58201

WA6LYY
Kirk D Williams
3501 28th Ave S
Grand Forks ND 58201

KA0GYU
Jerome T Albus
804 29th Ave S
Grand Forks ND 58201

KB0OBW
Bernardo P Dalan
820 29th Ave S
Grand Forks ND 58201

AC0AC
E. Alan Carter
2149 30th Ave S Apt 103
Grand Forks ND 582016503

KC0YWZ
Lance J Forst
2498 30th Ave S Apt 108
Grand Forks ND 58201

KB0OBU
Brian H Henderson
1850 34th St S 104
Grand Forks ND 58201

WB0SFE
Daniel N Erickson
607 3rd Ave S
Grand Forks ND 58201

KB0QZE
Mark C Kerr
815 40th Ave S E117
Grand Forks ND 58201

KB0STQ

John K Higganbotham
214 49th Ave S
Grand Forks ND 58201

KD0OMI
Spencer J Carmichael
803 49th Ave S
Grand Forks ND 58201

KB0LYD
James M Noss
1113 4th Ave N
Grand Forks ND 58203

N0TKP
Karen L Noss
1113 4th Ave N
Grand Forks ND 58203

KC0ICD
Patricia E Langwost
1619 4th Ave N
Grand Forks ND 58203

KC0ICG
Jeff R Vreeman
1621 4th Ave N
Grand Forks ND 58203

KE0A
Rodney B Klug
2012 4th Ave N
Grand Forks ND 582032919

WA0VMA
Earl S Mason
2211 4th Ave N
Grand Forks ND 58203

W0OGZ
Clifford J Thomforde
2615 4th Ave N
Grand Forks ND 58203

KC0GWM

Ron B Cole
7455 55th St S
Grand Forks ND 58201

N0JFD
Jamie E Chambers
5237 5th Ave N
Grand Forks ND 58203

AC0PT
Martin W Hynes
3106 5th Ave N 7
Grand Forks ND 58203

N6QDR
David C Mahlum
2014 6th Ave N
Grand Forks ND 58203

KB8LOD
Kris A Clingenpeel
2112 6th Ave N
Grand Forks ND 58203

KC0KKY
Spencer L Huhn
2609 6th Ave N
Grand Forks ND 58203

KD0RKL
Nicolai Baer
3512 6th Ave N
Grand Forks ND 58203

N0RNB
John C Nordlie
5406 6th Ave N
Grand Forks ND 58203

N0RNG
Theresa A Dangerfield
612 7th Ave N
Grand Forks ND 58203

WA0OWD

Janice W Sowokinos
3501 7th Ave N
Grand Forks ND 58201

KA0TBJ
Jonathan D Gerou
1409 8th Ave N
Grand Forks ND 58203

WA0K
Scott L Gingerich
5219 9th Ave N
Grand Forks ND 58203

KC0XW
James R Watt
902 Almonte Ave
Grand Forks ND 582014956

KB0OBV
Ronald W Oudean
1420 A Beech Dr
Grand Forks ND 58204

N0RNJ
Wayne R Westensee
Box 523
Grand Forks ND 58206

KC0YXF
Tom C Hansen
1015 Boyd Dr
Grand Forks ND 58203

KC0LUS
Melissa R Lembke
411A Brannon Hall Und
Grand Forks ND 58202

WA0VFY
David L Poppke
1418 Burntwood Ct
Grand Forks ND 58201

KC0ENE

Jonathon M Lentsch
719 Campbell Dr
Grand Forks ND 58201

Colt A Iseminger
917 Chestnut
Grand Forks ND 58201

KC0JBL
Chris A Richtsmeier
550 Carleton Ct 10
Grand Forks ND 58203

KD0NMK
Howard H Gladwin
263 Circle Hills Dr
Grand Forks ND 58201

KC0OMW
Drew A Holler
1518 Charwood Ct
Grand Forks ND 58201

N6SJN
Howard H Gladwin
263 Circle Hills Dr
Grand Forks ND 58201

N7AWM
James R Lowe
3720 Cherry H31
Grand Forks ND 58201

N0LLB
Leon F Osborne Jr
286 Circle Hills Dr
Grand Forks ND 58201

KD0IOD
Jeffrey D Manley
923 Cherry St
Grand Forks ND 58201

WB6LKL
Ernest E Anderson
273 Circle Hills Drive
Grand Forks ND 58201

W0JMW
Frederick W Pasbrig
110 Cherry St Apt 8
Grand Forks ND 58203

KD5OWQ
Sarah A Anderson
273 Circle Hills Drive
Grand Forks ND 58201

W0ARS
James R Lowe
3300 Cherry St Unit D141
Grand Forks ND 58201

K0IJI
Abraham F Muscari
214 Cleo Ct
Grand Forks ND 58201

KC0LUR
Richard D Shervold
3518 Cherry Ste D-9
Grand Forks ND 58201

N0INS
Alan H Meldrum
512 Columbia Rd N
Grand Forks ND 58201

KA0QMW
Gary R French
215 Chestnut
Grand Forks ND 58201

KA0GYR
Wayne A Stoltman
621 Cottonwood St
Grand Forks ND 58201

KD0AOC

KG0EK

Jeffrey M Awes
1025 Cottonwood St
Grand Forks ND 58201

KD0CEQ
Andrew F Gleich Jr
1720 Cottonwood St
Grand Forks ND 58201

KB9WOB
Kevin L Huyck
111 Cottonwood St 10
Grand Forks ND 58201

K0DCM
Keith H Johnson
1907 Drees Dr
Grand Forks ND 58201

KD7AZE
Garrick M Peterson
1508 Dyke Ave
Grand Forks ND 58203

AA0MY
Foy D Cox Jr
7696 E N Washington St
Grand Forks ND 58203

KC0PCZ
Timothy F Kraemer
2696 Fox Farm Rd
Grand Forks ND 58203

KC0MSW
Peter P Kraemer
2696 Fox Farm Rd
Grand Forks ND 58203

KC0CRU
Chris R Milford
6374 Gateway Dr
Grand Forks ND 58203

KB0YXO

John M Beaton
507 Gertrude Ave
Grand Forks ND 58201

WD0DEN
William G Little
2483 Glenwood Dr
Grand Forks ND 58201

KA0RKY
Oliver C Bertleson
2526 Glenwood Dr
Grand Forks ND 58201

KA0CAE
Glen A Olson
4905 Golden Gate Dr
Grand Forks ND 58203

KB0BUB
Sandra M Olson
4905 Golden Gate Drive
Grand Forks ND 58203

KC0IBF
Erik S Blevins
326 Hancock Hall
Grand Forks ND 58202

KB1TCI
Joshua V Nelson
510 Harvard St  Apartment 5
Grand Forks ND 58203

WB0VPC
Frank W Beaver Jr
4673 Homestead Cir
Grand Forks ND 58201

K0JMM
Merle J Mathison
2487 Huntington Park Dr
Grand Forks ND 582016136

WB0BMD

John H Waters III
6201 Lake Dr
Grand Forks ND 58201

KB0LXX
James D Campbell
6515 Lake Dr
Grand Forks ND 58201

KD0PBA
Scott A Foss
1133 Landeco Ln 115
Grand Forks ND 58201

K0PBA
Scott A Foss
1133 Landeco Ln 115
Grand Forks ND 58201

KD0MUD
Gregory R Plautz
3624 Landeco Ln 23B
Grand Forks ND 58201

KC0TIX
Tyson R Hammond
1133 Landeco Ln Apt 301
Grand Forks ND 58201

KC0TIW
Candice L Schmidt
1073 Landeco Ln Apt 7
Grand Forks ND 58201

KC0LKB
Stuart A Gott
3120 Legend Ln
Grand Forks ND 58201

KB0TJM
Bruce A Newland
4798 Lynbrook Ln
Grand Forks ND 58201

KF4IRM

Mark A Koponen
4709 Lynnbrook Ln
Grand Forks ND 58201

KC0TIZ
Sarah L Chelliah
3890 Mulberry Dr
Grand Forks ND 58201

KC0SKE
Noah J Chelliah Jr
3890 Mulberry Drive
Grand Forks ND 58201

KA0SVY
John F Schaffer
1701 N 3rd St
Grand Forks ND 58203

N0ZAT
Edward W Strenkowski
8001 N 52nd St
Grand Forks ND 582038816

KB0YRK
Mark A Rice
415 N 6th St
Grand Forks ND 58203

KC0CFQ
Cindy J Rice
415 N 6th St
Grand Forks ND 58203

N0QDT
Steven J Rowe
1412 N 1st St
Grand Forks ND 58203

KC0JEP
David M Schroeder
1015 N 39th St G-28
Grand Forks ND 58203

KC0PCY

Michael J Wuitschick
815 N 39th St 308G
Grand Forks ND 58203

KD0QQL
Logan A Gloss
815 N 39th St Apt 202F
Grand Forks ND 58203

KB0BTX
Thomas M Lockney Sr
1015 N 39th St F23
Grand Forks ND 58201

KB0BTY
Thomas M Lockney Jr
1015 N 39th St F23
Grand Forks ND 58201

KC0SKD
Donna M Schaffer
1701 N 3rd St
Grand Forks ND 58203

KF0XI
Leonard R Becker
405 N 3rd St Apt 9
Grand Forks ND 58203

KC0GHM
Blaise A Mibeck
715 N 40th 102 H
Grand Forks ND 58203

KC0LMN
Susan T Mibeck
715 N 40th St 102H
Grand Forks ND 58203

KA3KMW
John A Dennison
715 N 42nd St 203B
Grand Forks ND 58201

K0HXL

Jerry J Schaefer
932 N 4th St
Grand Forks ND 58203

KD0NML
Eric J Tweton
1817 N 4th St
Grand Forks ND 58203

KC0REN
Neil F Woolsey
1819 N 4th St
Grand Forks ND 58203

KC0YXG
Todd E Herz
1812 N 4th St
Grand Forks ND 58203

KB0PQT
Steven R Kamletz
314 N 4th St 2
Grand Forks ND 58201

KC0TIY
Gregory J Gust
565 N 5th St
Grand Forks ND 58203

N0QDU
John W Tracy
210 N 6th St Apt C 8
Grand Forks ND 58201

KB0FKK
Don C Nelson
210 N 9th 3
Grand Forks ND 58203

KF4ME
Mark A Koponen
1312 Noble Cove
Grand Forks ND 58201

KA0HDN

Richard R Wright
610 Oak St
Grand Forks ND 58201

KC0LMP
Dean D Smith
818 Oak St
Grand Forks ND 58201

N0LTE
William M Hollifield Jr
2703 Oak St
Grand Forks ND 58201

KB0YXL
Thomas C Ferguson
313 Park Ave
Grand Forks ND 58203

KC0LMO
Ryan M Kramer
1115 Park Dr 3
Grand Forks ND 58201

KF5FLO
Steven H Taylor
PO Box 14271
Grand Forks ND 58208

N6IFF
Mark H Foster
PO Box 7186
Grand Forks ND 582027186

N0PKD
Chad E Hopkins
3397 Primrose Court 107
Grand Forks ND 58201

KB0QWU
Cheryl M Kahlbaugh
3393 Primrose Ct 108
Grand Forks ND 58201

KB0HOD

Grant G Kahlbaugh
3393 Primrose Ct Apt 108
Grand Forks ND 58201

KB8ZXB
Adam C Deem
3383 Primrose Ct Apt C-10
Grand Forks ND 58201

KC0CFO
Robert E Hestbech
720 Promenade Ct
Grand Forks ND 58203

WB0YJZ
Thomas T Berge
1113 Reeves Dr
Grand Forks ND 58201

KC0NH
Robert A Johnson
1617 Rider Rd
Grand Forks ND 58201

W0GZD
Paul M Bossoletti
1648 Riverside Dr
Grand Forks ND 58201

K0STW
Scott T Williams
1834 S 20th St Apt 9
Grand Forks ND 58201

W0GFE
Vincent L Gangelhoff
2601 S 36th St
Grand Forks ND 58201

KG4BFW
Mark E Frazier
1343 S 38th St
Grand Forks ND 58201

KB1GIM

Matthew E Burton Kelly
21.5 S 4th St  Apt 5
Grand Forks ND 58201

KD4UIT
Karl L Mc Kinnon
308 S 5th St
Grand Forks ND 58201

N0ZGT
Noah N Chelliah
1191 S Columbia Rd
Grand Forks ND 58201

WB7OMY
Edgar D De Remer
2019 S 12 St
Grand Forks ND 58201

W0EUQ
Carol J Kraus
1822 S 17th St
Grand Forks ND 58201

W0EUQ
George E Kraus
1822 S 17th St
Grand Forks ND 58201

KC0LUP
Carol J Kraus
1822 S 17th St
Grand Forks ND 58201

KA0HSS
Michael C Hesterberg
2625 S 17th St 10
Grand Forks ND 58201

KD0FJS
Megan M Breitung
2904 S 17th St 303
Grand Forks ND 58202

KZ0GEM

Megan M Breitung
2904 S 17th St 303
Grand Forks ND 58202

KC0IDN
Raymond K Twedell
1014 S 19th St
Grand Forks ND 58201

KC0NPK
Brandon R Kasprowicz
1914 S 20th St Apt 32
Grand Forks ND 58201

KC0REJ
Angeline A Dufault
829 S 25th St 2
Grand Forks ND 58201

KC0HMF
Dennis A Goertzen
2200 S 29 St 72-S
Grand Forks ND 58201

N0ME
Don W Meissner
2225 S 34th St Apt 13
Grand Forks ND 58201

N0ELF
Don W Meissner
2225 S 34th St Apt 13
Grand Forks ND 58201

KC0FTH
Lowell P Stanlake
1715 S 35th St
Grand Forks ND 582015721

KB0DUY
Richard D Jurgens
1305 S 9th St
Grand Forks ND 58201

KD0RDH

Ne North Dakota Contest Club
1110 Sanford Rd 317
Grand Forks ND 58203

KC0NDF
Christopher A Sprenger
2800 Shadow Rd
Grand Forks ND 58201

KI0W
Larry R Holm
1011 Shakespeare Rd
Grand Forks ND 58203

K0LWT
Evan W Trosvik
1110 Stanford Rd 317
Grand Forks ND 58203

KC0UIT
Keith D Severson
1110 Stanford Rd Apt 212
Grand Forks ND 58203

N0NGW
Gerald H Nies
1815 University Ave
Grand Forks ND 58203

KG6TCE
Tadeusz J Kanski
4270 University Ave  304
Grand Forks ND 58203

KD0RMH
Bradley R Schanche
3904 University Ave Apt 13
Grand Forks ND 58203

KC0EWX
Sioux Amateur Radio Club
2901 University Ave Stop 8385
Memorial Union Rm 113
Grand Forks ND 58202

KC0FTD
David Rose
116B W Hall Und
Grand Forks ND 58202

KD0OMH
David P Masterson
2411 W Fallcreek Ct
Grand Forks ND 58201

K0RSA
Dennis L Coulter
3306 Walnut St
Grand Forks ND 582017667

W5WXR
Aaron D Kennedy
324 Walnut St
Grand Forks ND 58201

N0PKT
Allan A Puzianowski
313A Walsh Hall
Grand Forks ND 58202

KD0GVZ
Truman P Reed Jr
Grand Forks ND 58201

KD0IKG
Michael L Garritson
Grand Forks ND 58208

KC0JEQ
Jason D Bonice
Grand Forks ND 58208

N0VSH
David D Cook
Grand Forks ND 582040093

KD0MTD
Truman P Reed Jr
Grand Forks ND 582065905

KC0JPP
Gary Garritson
Grand Forks ND 582082413

KC0LUQ
Stacy L Bjornstad
Grand Forks ND 582084003

N0GF
Greater Grand Forks Ares
Grand Forks ND 582084773

## FCC Amateur Radio Licenses in Grand Forks AFB

KB0MIE
David G Warner
14190 Beech Ave
Grand Forks AFB ND 58204

KB0DSX
Levi A Gholson
1390B Beech Ave
Grand Forks AFB ND 58204

KQ0R
Robert E Concannon Jr
1606 Hickam Dr
Grand Forks AFB ND 58204

KC5PIP
Robert E Concannon Jr
1606 Hickam Dr
Grand Forks AFB ND 58204

KC0IBG
James E Steidel
1765-B Iowa St
Grand Forks AFB ND 58204

N0ICE
James E Steidel
1765 Iowa St Unit B
Grand Forks AFB ND 58204

KB0VFI
Paul D La Scola
1502 B J St
Grand Forks AFB ND 58204

N7FWH
Milton A Meinhardt
1512B March Ave
Grand Forks AFB ND 58205

KD0DAW
Adam C Deem
1451 Nevada Dr Unit A
Grand Forks AFB ND 58205

KB7FLD
Eric V Brown
PSC Box 2756
Grand Forks AFB ND 58207

N0RNE
Geoffrey A Brown
PSC Bx 4555
Grand Forks AFB ND 58207

KB0ZMO
Anthony M Dickens
Grand Forks AFB ND 58207

KB0VYC
Military Vhf Society
Grand Forks AFB ND 582040093

## FCC Amateur Radio Licenses in Grandin

N0NRV
James N Dueker
16187 13 R St SE
Grandin ND 58038

KA0WNN
Paul C Setnes
Box 183
Grandin ND 58038

## FCC Amateur Radio Licenses in Granville

KD0ASL
Raymond C Lilliquist
5587 15th Ave N
Granville ND 587419578

KB6DND
Mary E Robinette
506 W Ave SW
Granville ND 587414105

KF6XO
Paul P Robinette Jr
506 W Ave SW
Granville ND 587414105

## FCC Amateur Radio Licenses in Grassy Butte

KA0RYQ
Jeff C Tachenko
Hc 4 Box 33
Grassy Butte ND 58634

## FCC Amateur Radio Licenses in Grenora

N0TWZ
Thomas R Enander
Grenora ND 58845

## FCC Amateur Radio Licenses in Halliday

W0NDK
Larry A Benjamin
8205 2nd St NW
Halliday ND 58636

KB0VRH
Larry A Benjamin

8205 2nd St NW
Halliday ND 58636

WD0DAG
Marvin Synnes
1269 95th Ave SW
Halliday ND 58636

## FCC Amateur Radio Licenses in Hamilton

KB0TJP
Lawrence E Collins
9108 151st Ave NE
Hamilton ND 58238

WA0AA
Wesley A Argue
Hamilton ND 58238

## FCC Amateur Radio Licenses in Hannaford

KB0BRR
Denise M Beaver-Eslinger
750 105th Ave SE
Hannaford ND 584489406

K0DHB
Arnold J Gronneberg
Rr 1 Box 79
Hannaford ND 58448

## FCC Amateur Radio Licenses in Harvey

KE6LYS
Jerrilynn M Peterson
4317 30th St NE
Harvey ND 58341

KQ6AF
Robert L Peterson
4317 30th St NE
Harvey ND 58341

KA7UEJ
Marlin G Meharry
921 Adams St
Harvey ND 58341

AB9EU
John M Bell
524 Judy Blvd
Harvey ND 58341

KC0DTS
Ronald R Reimche
125 W Brewster St
Harvey ND 58341

## FCC Amateur Radio Licenses in Harwood

N0WQW
Harvey J Hirning
5602 53rd Ave N
Harwood ND 58042

KB0AZG
Debra A Anderson
8906 56th Ave N
Harwood ND 58048

KA0OBZ
Ernest G Jury
131 Bender Ln
Harwood ND 58042

KB0GHH
William M Bugbee
Rr 1 Box 17
Harwood ND 58042

N0JXO
Andrew C Zimmerman
Route 1 Box 539
Harwood ND 58042

KG0FR

Mark B Kerkvliet
507 Wally St
Harwood ND 58042

N0TEG
Katy A Kerkvliet
507 Wally St
Harwood ND 58042

## FCC Amateur Radio Licenses in Hatton

WA0CSK
Donald L Carlson
Rr 2 Box 47
Hatton ND 58240

W0HSR
Cornelius A Thompson
803 Jersey Ave
Hatton ND 58240

WA0CSL
Mary L Carlson
809 Spruce Ave
Hatton ND 58240

## FCC Amateur Radio Licenses in Hazen

WA0SUF
Lyle D Kruckenberg
4601 3rd St NW
Hazen ND 58545

K0GCC
Bernard W Teske
1010 Elm Rd Rte 3
Hazen ND 58545

N0YCE
Myron K Heinemeyer
1001 Fayette Drive
Hazen ND 58545

K6KL
Robert L Nelson
816 Mannhaven St
Hazen ND 58545

---

**FCC Amateur Radio Licenses in Hebron**

KD0QLE
Andrew J Maershbecker
Hebron ND 58638

KD0QZX
Leroy R Thomas
Hebron ND 58638

---

**FCC Amateur Radio Licenses in Hensel**

W0GOD
Linwood W Heironimus Jr
118 S Canton Ave
Hensel ND 58241

---

**FCC Amateur Radio Licenses in Hensler**

N0IYM
Francis W Wetzstein
HC 2
Hensler ND 585470169

---

**FCC Amateur Radio Licenses in Hettinger**

KA0BAW
Duane L Boyce
105 2nd St N
Hettinger ND 58639

KD0PPO
Wade A Howard
104 7th St N
Hettinger ND 58639

KA0BOA
Philip R Resner
104 9th Ave N
Hettinger ND 58639

W0VWJ
Palmer B Forsmoe
Hettinger ND 58639

---

**FCC Amateur Radio Licenses in Hillsboro**

KD0BVF
Jakob Hurt
612 Loyal Ave
Hillsboro ND 58045

KD0BVG
Leslie M Hurt
612 Loyal Ave
Hillsboro ND 58045

---

**FCC Amateur Radio Licenses in Hoople**

WB0VWW
Maynard L Rieger
Hoople ND 58243

---

**FCC Amateur Radio Licenses in Horace**

K0GJS
Donald D Goerger
701 3rd St E
Horace ND 580470249

KD0GHW
Russell H Sahr
6705 76th Ave S
Horace ND 58047

KC0FHG
Carlo R Samson

6912 81 Ave S
Horace ND 58047

N0RF
Joseph M Gregg
114 Apple Ln
Horace ND 58047

N0LG
Linda L Gregg
114 Apple Ln
Horace ND 58047

W0ZOK
Gene L Wicklund
10213 CR 17 S
Horace ND 58047

KD0GWB
John C Wicklund
10213 CR 17 S
Horace ND 58047

KD0GWC
Ross F Wicklund
10213 CR 17 S
Horace ND 58047

KB0DTW
Diane M Wicklund
10213 CR 17 S
Horace ND 58047

KD0ACC
Ginger R Erickson
4854 CR 81 S
Horace ND 58047

KD0ACD
Trevor B Erickson
4854 CR 81 S
Horace ND 58047

KD0GWA
Quinn E Olson

148 Ironwood Dr
Horace ND 58047

KA0LDG
Kent R Olson
148 Ironwood Dr
Horace ND 580474002

N0NRX
Brent R Wasem
602 Sheyenne Dr
Horace ND 580474427

KC0WIS
Dean H Moen
313 Southwood Dr
Horace ND 58047

K0WZ
Dean H Moen
313 Southwood Dr
Horace ND 58047

KC0OET
Kory J Peterson
414 Southwood Dr
Horace ND 58047

KC0DCG
Jay R French
7405 Sunnyside St
Horace ND 58047

## FCC Amateur Radio Licenses in Inkster

KB0FWB
Gary L Bornsen
Rt 2 Box 39
Inkster ND 58244

## FCC Amateur Radio Licenses in Jamestown

N0SRP

Claudia E Bollinger
1604 10 Ave NE
Jamestown ND 58401

N0HNM
Lyle F Bollinger
1604 10th Ave NE
Jamestown ND 58401

KB0YNS
Alan T Rinehart
1122 11th Ave SE
Jamestown ND 58401

KA0TVE
James H Gackle
1412 11th St SW
Jamestown ND 58401

N0SOW
Ardith M Kleingartner
106 12th Ave NE
Jamestown ND 58401

KB0OCC
John J Kubenski Sr
1102 12th Ave SE
Jamestown ND 58401

KA0ZEB
Cheryl L Kane
1108 12th St NE 2
Jamestown ND 58401

KA0EGC
Dennis C Kane
1108 12th St NE Apt 2
Jamestown ND 58401

KG0FW
John M Black
1111 12th St SE
Jamestown ND 58401

KC0NQR

Paul G Bensch
337 13 Ave NE
Jamestown ND 58401

N0GUZ
Charles V Wells
1003 13 Ave SW
Jamestown ND 58401

N0HOW
Timothy G Mc Carty
1404 13th Ave SW
Jamestown ND 58401

WA0EKT
Floyd F Schauer
301 15th Ave NE
Jamestown ND 58401

W0EOZ
Arthur F Jensen
1006 16th St SW
Jamestown ND 584015326

KC0TJA
Shane P Burkle
1411 16th St SW
Jamestown ND 58401

N0USK
Thomas D Kleingartner
1002 19th St NE
Jamestown ND 58401

AB0HH
Ronnie L Omsberg
237 23rd Ave NE
Jamestown ND 58401

KC0ASM
Thomas A Simpson
714 2nd Ave NE
Jamestown ND 58401

KC0GCJ

Jason J Linz
1122 2nd Ave NW
Jamestown ND 58401

KC0LAC
Michelle L Vee
1122 2nd Ave NW
Jamestown ND 58401

WB0TYQ
Kenneth R Wade
8381 32 R St SE
Jamestown ND 58401

KB0QDJ
Andrew I Hennessey
8375 33rd St SE
Jamestown ND 58401

KA0TVD
Francis H Simmers
9054 37th St SE
Jamestown ND 58401

N0ZKE
Patrick D Bennett
7781 38 St SE
Jamestown ND 58401

WB0TYP
Theresa A Haag Grubbs
711 3rd Ave NE
Jamestown ND 584013333

KB0RSB
Cecil J Roth Jr
1706 3rd Ave NE
Jamestown ND 584012419

KC0BBX
Anthony C Roth
1706 3rd Ave NE
Jamestown ND 584012419

K0RKY

Clyde J Grubbs Jr
505 3rd Ave SE
Jamestown ND 58401

KA0HOI
Jean F Grubbs
505 3rd Ave SE
Jamestown ND 58401

W0LAZ
Harry A Mason
814 3rd St NE
Jamestown ND 58401

K0EPV
De Wayne E Doyle
316 4th Ave SW
Jamestown ND 58401

KA0ZEQ
Patrick J Tobin
2009 4th St NE
Jamestown ND 58401

N0KGY
Sarah A Tobin
2009 4th St NE
Jamestown ND 58401

W0WT
Warren J Tobin
2009 4th St NE
Jamestown ND 584013926

KC0NQQ
Agnes R Jensen
1401 5 Ave SE Apt 5
Jamestown ND 58401

K0HPG
William Rath Jr
1507 5th Ave NE
Jamestown ND 58401

N0SND

Franklin J Balak Jr
318 5th Ave SE
Jamestown ND 58401

KB0LWZ
Marcus R Jensen
1401 5th Ave SE 5
Jamestown ND 58401

KB0LXK
Jason S Jensen
1401 5th Ave SE Apt 5
Jamestown ND 58401

W0AZV
Kurt Hall
2012 5th St NE
Jamestown ND 58401

WB0TWN
Robert W Todd
1519 6th Ave NE
Jamestown ND 58401

W0FX
Jamestown Amateur Radio Club
205 6th St SE
Jamestown ND 58401

AA0LU
Allura M Sortland
3725 85 R Ave SE
Jamestown ND 584019109

W0JYD
Erle K Sortland
3725 85 R Ave SE
Jamestown ND 584019109

KB0BRS
La Verne R Schelske
1815 8th Ave NE
Jamestown ND 58401

W0IBZ

Ron B Cruff Jr
404 8th Ave SE
Jamestown ND 58401

KC0QEN
Mark A Deery
503 8th Ave SE
Jamestown ND 584014453

K0TIN
Warren R Larson
708 8th Ave SE
Jamestown ND 58401

WD0HPZ
Noel E Mc Coy
907 9th Ave SW
Jamestown ND 58401

N0NOH
Charles H Simmons
1405 9th Ave SW
Jamestown ND 58401

KA0VWM
Jason R Flynn
Rr 1 Box 107 Bloom Township
Jamestown ND 58401

KA0VWO
Virginia S Templeton
Rural Rt 1 Box 107 Bloom Township
Jamestown ND 58401

KB0VWU
Michael J Mc Cormick
Rr 1 Box 278B
Jamestown ND 58401

KA0TNL
Rollie M Hill
Rr 5 Box 39
Jamestown ND 58401

KB0LWY

Irene L Simmers
Route 1 Box 68
Jamestown ND 58401

N0XRT
Michael D Schlecht
105 E  Rokiwan Rd
Jamestown ND 58401

N0TXA
Robert C Wells
3945 Highway 281 SE
Jamestown ND 58401

KA0ZEC
Jeffrey A Schrader
502 Holiday Park Village
Jamestown ND 58401

W0ODR
Jeffrey A Schrader
502 Holiday Park Village
Jamestown ND 58401

N0ZKD
Grant S Schmidt
937 Western Park
Jamestown ND 58401

KC0WMG
Sibyl K Hines
1419 Western Park Village
Jamestown ND 58401

KB0BRP
Enrique Alvarez III
Jamestown ND 58402

KB0BRQ
Enrique Alvarez II
Jamestown ND 58402

KC0LAB
Matthew D Opsahl
Jamestown ND 584021435

## FCC Amateur Radio Licenses in Kathryn

N0MAF
Janice R Arneson
Rr 2 Box 37
Kathryn ND 58049

N0KGW
Ernest A Arneson
Rt 2 Box 37
Kathryn ND 58049

N0SRM
Paul E Fritchie
345 Oak Ave
Kathryn ND 58049

## FCC Amateur Radio Licenses in Kenmare

KB0MTI
David B Cuthbertson
615 E Division
Kenmare ND 58746

KC0NPU
Ronald B Martinsen
Kenmare ND 58746

## FCC Amateur Radio Licenses in Kensal

N0TEO
Todd S Kollman
901 81st Rural Ave SE
Kensal ND 58455

N0XHF
Julie A Kollman
Rr 1 Box 68
Kensal ND 58455

N0XRZ

Scott A Kollman
207 Parker St
Kensal ND 58455

## FCC Amateur Radio Licenses in Killdeer

KA0AZC
Cheryl A Bakken
Hcr 2 Box 11Bb
Killdeer ND 58640

## FCC Amateur Radio Licenses in Kindred

WA0KTL
Donald E Strand
5495 156 Ave SE
Kindred ND 580519501

WA0KTM
Betty Lou Strand
5495 156 Ave SE
Kindred ND 580519501

W0FVG
Ernest W Nettum
RFD 1
Kindred ND 58051

## FCC Amateur Radio Licenses in Kulm

KB3IXT
Benjamin Scheirer
106 1st Ave SW
Kulm ND 58456

## FCC Amateur Radio Licenses in Lakota

KB0BHZ
Lloyd O Craft
509 2nd St W

Lakota ND 58344

KA0FIN
Warren W Westensee
Box 283
Lakota ND 58344

## FCC Amateur Radio Licenses in Lamoure

W7IHU
Arthur R Fick
310 1st St N W
Lamoure ND 58458

N0JCT
Barney Isakson
221 4th St NE
Lamoure ND 58458

KB0BWL
Phyllis J Arth
Evergreen Trailer Ct 6
Lamoure ND 58458

## FCC Amateur Radio Licenses in Langdon

KC0VDB
Charles J Miller
1208 11th St
Langdon ND 58249

KC0YKS
Charles J Miller
1208 11th St
Langdon ND 58249

KF4NFF
Lisa M Heironimus
210 13th Ave
Langdon ND 58249

KA0BKO
Ronald L Muhs

1321 5th St
Langdon ND 58249

KE4UFJ
Linwood W Heironimus Jr
8550 Hwy 1
Langdon ND 58249

KB0SRA
Weslie L Franchuk
Langdon ND 58249

## FCC Amateur Radio Licenses in Lankin

WB0QFS
Paul E Hodny
5870 122 Ave NE
Lankin ND 58250

## FCC Amateur Radio Licenses in Lansford

KE6VZS
Dale I Gregory Sr
Lansford ND 587500057

## FCC Amateur Radio Licenses in Larimore

WA0ZLZ
Jordell O Brose
2030 36 St
Larimore ND 58251

KC0VWM
David W Mcshane
1395 41st St NE
Larimore ND 58251

N0RNL
Marlen E Rustebakke
2563 42nd St NE
Larimore ND 58251

KC0HVH
Nancy M Byrd
320 Booth
Larimore ND 58251

KB0LXY
Eric K Peterson
724 Terry Ave
Larimore ND 58251

N0DVF
Ronald P Flynn
317 Towner Ave
Larimore ND 58251

KB0QWO
Michael T Grant
321 W Main
Larimore ND 58251

AA0WU
Michael E Crouse
Larimore ND 58251

KB0QWX
John E Logan
Larimore ND 58251

N0KXO
Charlotte M Grant
Larimore ND 58251

## FCC Amateur Radio Licenses in Lawton

W0JBM
James B Thorson
8 4th Ave N
Lawton ND 58345

## FCC Amateur Radio Licenses in Leeds

KC0HXS
A Sanfrid Anderson

6160 52 Ave SE
Leeds ND 58346

KC0FDK
Kevin C Lunde
Leeds ND 583460372

## FCC Amateur Radio Licenses in Lehr

N0NVQ
Everett E Hoard
403 S Mc Intosh St
Lehr ND 58460

W0HPS
Everett E Hoard
403 S Mc Intosh St
Lehr ND 58460

## FCC Amateur Radio Licenses in Leonard

KD0PBB
Wade Stine
14886 53rd St SE
Leonard ND 58052

KB0VSX
Wade Stine
14886 53rd St SE
Leonard ND 58052

WB0NNC
Roland W Heuer
15115 58 St SE
Leonard ND 58052

WB0VRO
Duane Reistad
15370 59th St SE
Leonard ND 58052

## FCC Amateur Radio Licenses in Lidgerwood

W0GQC
Gene F Garcia
126 4th Ave NE
Lidgerwood ND 580530445

KA0SNW
Robert F Knaust Sr
129 4th Ave NE
Lidgerwood ND 58053

## FCC Amateur Radio Licenses in Lignite

KC0AQN
Marlyn J Brorby
Lignite ND 58752

## FCC Amateur Radio Licenses in Lincoln

KB0NJG
Eric R Wanchic
110 Allen Dr
Lincoln ND 58504

KB0LEO
Donald D Carley
3 Brevet
Lincoln ND 58504

W0KRC
Donald D Carley
3 Brevet
Lincoln ND 58504

KB0QZA
Robert W Johnston
21 Carlin Dr
Lincoln ND 58504

N0SIB
Milton D Broeckel
19 Mc Dougal Dr
Lincoln ND 58504

N0XMN
Richard J Rhoades
36 Mc Dougall Dr
Lincoln ND 58504

W0DLT
Daryl L Tietz
4 Santee Rd
Lincoln ND 58504

## FCC Amateur Radio Licenses in Linton

KA0RBM
Raylene M Henkelmann
Linton ND 58552

WD8PDI
Frederick W Henkelmann
Linton ND 58552

## FCC Amateur Radio Licenses in Lisbon

N0BQY
Herman C Funk
13250 65th St SE
Lisbon ND 58054

KA0RPY
Harry A Stamnes
312 7th Ave W
Lisbon ND 58054

WB0FDV
Francis H Zeck Jr
502 Lincoln
Lisbon ND 58054

N0WUL
Willard L Kelsen
405 Oak St Box 73
Lisbon ND 58054

K0MBL

Asle K Lewis
820 Pine Ridge Drive
Lisbon ND 580544047

KC0EXW
John L Easterday
1112 Webster St
Lisbon ND 58054

## FCC Amateur Radio Licenses in Litchville

KC0QEM
Janet L Lighthill-Ridley
5343 106th Ave SE
Litchville ND 584619703

KD0MMM
John T Baumgartner
5041 107 Ave SE
Litchville ND 58461

KC0FGH
Jeremy J Zeltinger
10232 44th St SE
Litchville ND 58461

KC0KCU
Katrina M Zeltinger
10232 44th St SE
Litchville ND 58461

KC0ZWN
Ethan I Zeltinger
10232 44th Wt SE
Litchville ND 58461

W0PVG
Norman W Colebank
301 6th Ave
Litchville ND 58461

## FCC Amateur Radio Licenses in Maddock

KB0CCV
Michael J Sorlie
4776 41st NE
Maddock ND 58348

KA0ZZA
David D Sorlie
4776 41st St NE
Maddock ND 58348

N0JCB
Rita S Sorlie
4776 41st St NE
Maddock ND 58348

KC7FTW
Larry E Van Dolah Sr
3678 42nd Ave NE
Maddock ND 58348

KB0MWZ
Jon B Hermanson
4915 50th Ave NE
Maddock ND 58348

KA0ZUX
Jay Rice
Box 272
Maddock ND 58348

N0BG
Benson County Amateur Radio Club
4850 Hwy 30
Maddock ND 58348

KF0HR
Teran W Hermanson
4850 Hwy 30
Maddock ND 58348

KC0LBL
Benson County Arc
4850 Hwy 30
Maddock ND 58348

KA0WHG
Dawn M Hermanson
4850 Hwy 30
Maddock ND 583489530

KI0DW
Bryan C Kenner
301 Lincoln Ave
Maddock ND 58348

W0PUP
Jay Rice
Maddock ND 58348

KB0ACA
Dean K Sorlie
Maddock ND 58348

N0WAT
Marjorie G Rice
Maddock ND 58348

KB0MWX
Norman O Haagenstad
Maddock ND 583480163

N0HWT
Norman D Haugen
Maddock ND 583480306

---

**FCC Amateur Radio Licenses in Mandan**

KB0OXW
Nickolette L Keller
201.5 Division St NW
Mandan ND 58554

KC0MN
Larry N Dale
2604 10th Ave NW
Mandan ND 58554

KB0YLV
Douglas E Arneson Mr

1200 10th Ave SE
Mandan ND 58554

921 27th St NW
Mandan ND 58554

KC0COH
Cordell J Booke
502 11 St NW
Mandan ND 58554

W0GHQ
Eugene W Finz
910 2nd Ave NW
Mandan ND 58554

KC0ZWM
Tanner R Kahl
1112 11th St SE
Mandan ND 58554

KB0QZF
Audrey L Ruck
1210 2nd St SW
Mandan ND 58554

KB1BYP
Jeff S Bradford
701 16th Ave NW
Mandan ND 58554

WB0WPD
Darlene M Hagerott
3255 31st Ave
Mandan ND 585548120

KB0QYT
Stephen W Conmy
1409 16th St SE
Mandan ND 58554

KB4AA
Phillip M Walker
3405 37th St NW
Mandan ND 58554

KB0OXX
Christal M Orgaard
811.5 1st Ave NW
Mandan ND 58554

WB0CW
Phillip M Walker
3405 37th St NW
Mandan ND 58554

K6STS
Douglas G Niessen
4201 21st St SE Apt 308
Mandan ND 58554

K0VX
Phillip M Walker
3405 37th St NW
Mandan ND 58554

N0JMA
Steve Koppy
4536 23rd Ave
Mandan ND 58554

N0SDB
Timothy P Rasset
4109 38th Ave NW
Mandan ND 58554

N0JMB
Francie M Koppy
4536 23rd Ave
Mandan ND 58554

K0CMS
Jeffrey B Strange
2075 38th St
Mandan ND 58554

KA0GVJ
Norman O Ravnaas

KC0TSU
Malcolm D Macbeth

600 3rd Ave SE
Mandan ND 58554

K0TMH
Harold L Parkin
131 3rd Ave SE 201
Mandan ND 58554

N0LZK
James A Munns
800 4 Ave NE
Mandan ND 58554

KC0HXG
Richard D Hansen
2801 40th Ave SE Unit 104
Mandan ND 58554

KB0IIX
Dennis J Connelly
2904 46th Ave SE
Mandan ND 58554

KB0FVV
Wayne M Doll
2905 46th Ave SE
Mandan ND 58554

N0RYC
Joy C Doll
2905 46th Ave SE
Mandan ND 58554

KC0LUO
Sarah E Rothschiller
1405 4th St NW
Mandan ND 58554

W0OJZ
Roy F Isaksen
711 5th St NW
Mandan ND 585542510

KB0ALD
Jim P Renner

1800 6th Ave NW
Mandan ND 58554

KB3DHC
Alan W Stumpf
1201 6th St NW
Mandan ND 58554

KB0QZH
Kenneth G Helmer
1408 7th Ave SE
Mandan ND 58554

KD0RET
Leeann J Thorstenson
401 7th St NW
Mandan ND 58554

W0ADM
Christopher G Boehm
1308 7th St NW
Mandan ND 58554

KB0VOA
Gery P De Greef
101 9th Ave NW
Mandan ND 58554

W0HQC
Arnold L Edinger
703 9th Ave NW
Mandan ND 58554

AB0DX
Damon M Wolff
2208 9th Ave SE
Mandan ND 58554

N0JQJ
George J Caussyn
1500 Anns Pl 2
Mandan ND 58554

KB0CIB
Rick E Kalvoda

Rr 2 Box 22
Mandan ND 58554

216 Lake St
Mandan ND 58554

KD0GTF
Keith Ebel
4610 Cortez Cir
Mandan ND 58554

N0RYH
Le Roy K Kuntz
107 Linton Ave
Mandan ND 58554

N0YCT
Joe Kalvoda
2262 CR 138
Mandan ND 58554

KA0PDK
Nyla B Schock
1710 Monte Dr
Mandan ND 58554

N0JLZ
Mary Ann Kalvoda
2262 CR 138
Mandan ND 585548506

KB0CLV
Daniel J Miller
3663 Palomino Dr N
Mandan ND 58554

KB0LDE
Peter D Harriman
413 E Prairie
Mandan ND 58554

KC0ZWL
James P Bernhardt
709 Paulsen Dr
Mandan ND 58554

KC0MNC
James O Hanson
815 Elm St
Mandan ND 58554

WB0NZZ
Nels T Hagerott
Box 94 R 1
Mandan ND 58554

KC0MND
Randy J Zachmeier
2903 Hwy 1806 N
Mandan ND 585545319

KC0BUE
Michael R Moore
3201 Sandy Ln SE
Mandan ND 58554

N0POK
Chris E Albin
1301 John S Drive
Mandan ND 58554

WD0DYG
Gerald J Haider
1204 Sunset Dr
Mandan ND 58554

N0MBG
Denis J Mohn
3125 Ken St N
Mandan ND 58554

KC0LWN
George Kwitka
1810 Sunset Dr
Mandan ND 58554

KD0BTU
Dewey C Trehus

KC0TLL
Leroy K Kuntz

109 W Deer St
Mandan ND 58554

N0RYH
Leroy K Kuntz
109 W Deer St
Mandan ND 58554

N0VWY
Thomas P Axtmann
5016 Wagon Wheel Circle
Mandan ND 58554

NC0Z
Douglas C Jahner
3905 Waterfront Place
Mandan ND 58554

KB0LEY
Dreux C H Kautzmann
Mandan ND 58554

## FCC Amateur Radio Licenses in Manning

KD0AAL
David W Watkins
10348 16th St SW
Manning ND 58642

## FCC Amateur Radio Licenses in Manvel

WA8FAO
Michael B Celmer
Rr 1 Box 111B
Manvel ND 58256

## FCC Amateur Radio Licenses in Marion

KA0ENW
Leslie A Krenz
305 3rd Main St
Marion ND 58466

## FCC Amateur Radio Licenses in Marmarth

N0LWZ
Lori J Eagon
16907 86th St SW
Marmarth ND 586439268

KB0CFG
Gary L Bagley
Box 86
Marmarth ND 58643

N0AUR
Patsy L Rocki
Marmarth ND 58643

## FCC Amateur Radio Licenses in Max

KL7JFH
Du Wayne J Bostow
302 Carvell St
Max ND 58759

KC0PGC
Patti L Walth
Max ND 587590162

KB0VOB
Otto J Walth
Max ND 587590162

## FCC Amateur Radio Licenses in Maxbass

KB0SNE
Michael L House
1810 CR 20 NW
Maxbass ND 58760

KA0WWP
Joel I Erickson
1850 CR 30
Maxbass ND 587609790

## FCC Amateur Radio Licenses in Mayville

KC0GV
Stuart L Neset
115 1st Ave NW
Mayville ND 58257

K0RJ
Eugene G Krause
129 3rd St SW
Mayville ND 582571344

KA0EDC
Delbert J Hlavinka
44 4 Ave SE
Mayville ND 58257

KA0EDD
Craig A Bye
29 4th Ave NE
Mayville ND 582571225

KA0CVR
Jeffrey W Lindaas
Rt 2 Box 90 A
Mayville ND 58257

KA0ZIM
Naomi C Lindaas
Rrt 2 Box 91
Mayville ND 58257

W0KZU
Elroy N Lindaas
Rt 2 Box 91
Mayville ND 58257

K0DHD
Neil A Gryte
42 Westwood Dr Rr 1
Mayville ND 58257

KA0EDB

Alvin T Tollefsrud
Mayville ND 58257

N0JCU
Roy H Coffin
Mayville ND 582570395

## FCC Amateur Radio Licenses in McClusky

N0UXL
Ardith M Kleingartner
350 1st Ave NW
McClusky ND 58463

N0SOW
Bert Kleingartner
Hc 1 Box 18A
McClusky ND 58463

## FCC Amateur Radio Licenses in McHenry

WX0O
Duane A Cunningham
8651 14th St NE
McHenry ND 584649205

N0SDA
Mabel C Cunningham
8651 14th St NE
McHenry ND 58464

KC0DJB
Keith E Edlund
1940 92nd Ave NE
McHenry ND 58464

## FCC Amateur Radio Licenses in McKenzie

KC0ZWQ
Lyndon J Mclean
7851 262nd St NE
McKenzie ND 58572

## FCC Amateur Radio Licenses in McVille

KB0NJH
Stephen M Braun
2431 109th Ave NE
McVille ND 58254

K0FUP
Donald H Schroeder
PO Box 24
McVille ND 58254

N0TAR
Arlan K Lilleoien
McVille ND 58254

## FCC Amateur Radio Licenses in Medina

KD0QVN
Duane F Bohnsack
521 School St SE
Medina ND 58467

## FCC Amateur Radio Licenses in Medora

N0KVH
Hallie Lavelle
Medora ND 58645

N0MGP
Joan L Jurgens
Medora ND 58645

## FCC Amateur Radio Licenses in Melville

KA0LIN
Wanda M Rath
Rt 3 Box 34
Melville ND 58421

## FCC Amateur Radio Licenses in Mercer

W0XZ
Herbert R Leupp
207 Wing St
Mercer ND 585590095

## FCC Amateur Radio Licenses in Milnor

N0XYK
Mark R Crider
320 1st St S
Milnor ND 580600233

N0SHL
Mitchel D Kjar
214 3rd St
Milnor ND 58060

N0SCS
George D Marquette
222 6th St
Milnor ND 58060

N0ASA
Hans G Hansen
Box 373
Milnor ND 58060

N0XHG
Jason R Marquette
Box 8
Milnor ND 58060

## FCC Amateur Radio Licenses in Minnewaukan

KB0MWU
Rick L Tofsrud
6250 48th St NE
Minnewaukan ND 58351

KB0MWY
Mark J Motis
701 B Ave S
Minnewaukan ND 58351

KB9VNB
Michael J Kostrewa
Minnewaukan ND 58351

KB9YUE
Mark J Olson
Minnewaukan ND 58351

## FCC Amateur Radio Licenses in Minot

KB0MRB
Aaron A Klingbeil
1120 1 St NE
Minot ND 58701

KB0DSV
Thomas K Wallace
711 10 St NE
Minot ND 58703

KB0UWL
Robert J Boschert
1400 100 Ave NW
Minot ND 58703

WA7ILR
Wallace C Rampy
409 10th Ave NE
Minot ND 58701

W0OAM
David A Van Gorkom
3205 10th St  SW  Apt A 11
Minot ND 58701

AB0ZB
Gary T Schroeder
523 10th St NE
Minot ND 58703

KB0RLV
Travis J Van Dyke
305 10th St SE
Minot ND 58701

KC0MMR
Chris A Kroetch
1912 10th St NW
Minot ND 58703

WA0LXB
Jesse G Weiss
1836 10th St SW
Minot ND 58701

WM0M
Larry Halton
3222 10th St SW
Minot ND 587017324

N0HYH
Richard C Schmidt
1501 111th St SE
Minot ND 587012632

K0RHS
Bishop Ryan High School Radio Club
316 11th Ave NW
Minot ND 58703

KD5TDY
James N Fisher
1508 11th St SE
Minot ND 58701

K0WVL
Jimmy R Mackey
1711 12 St SW
Minot ND 58701

KD0DY
Brian L Johnson
430 12th St NW
Minot ND 58703

KB0CVX
David R Dunsmoor
1608 13 St SW
Minot ND 58701

KC0NUV
Kevin R Slater
409 13th Ave NE
Minot ND 58703

KC0DYW
Scott M Wirtz
226 13th Ave SE
Minot ND 58701

KD4POJ
Dwayne E Lipscomb Sr
4201 13th St NE
Minot ND 58703

KE4ZLS
Carol M Lipscomb
4201 13th St NE
Minot ND 58703

NT0AF
Northern Tier Amateur Radio Club
4201 13th St NE
Minot ND 58703

KE0WA
William R Mahowald
1626 14 Ave SW
Minot ND 58701

WD0ALD
Paul A Krueger
5116 14th St SE
Minot ND 58701

KB0STM
Beverly A Cushing
817 15 1/2 Ave SW
Minot ND 58701

N0GC
Gerald A Cushing
817 15 1/2 Ave SW
Minot ND 58701

KB0CVY
Duane W Aase
914 15 1/2 Ave SW
Minot ND 58701

KC0VSB
Bruce I Christianson
1421 15th St SW
Minot ND 587015796

KC0WGE
Bruce I Christianson
1421 15th St SW
Minot ND 587015796

W0PGM
Bruce I Christianson
1421 15th St SW
Minot ND 587015796

KC0RBI
Magic City Qrp Club
400 16th Ave SW
Minot ND 58701

W0JER
Magic City Qrp Club
400 16th Ave SW
Minot ND 58701

K0TUP
Faye J Nelson
400 16th Ave SW
Minot ND 58701

W0TUP
Arlon F Nelson
400 16th Ave SW
Minot ND 58701

KC0WCI
Rebecca K Sundhagen
1604 16th St NW
Minot ND 58703

KA0NMX
Larry N Johnson
1315 17th Ave NW
Minot ND 58703

WA0EDF
Wayne J Holdeman
619 17th Ave SE
Minot ND 587016755

KC0UZN
Ian J Kenny
400 18th Ave SE Apt 15
Minot ND 58701

KB0AYX
Roberta K Bossie
512 18th St NW
Minot ND 58703

KB0AYY
Michael P Bossie
512 18th St NW
Minot ND 58703

KC0KHP
Cory R Hansen
1500 18th St SW 34
Minot ND 58701

KC0OAA
Kimberly A Hatch
2400 19th Ave NW
Minot ND 58703

N0IK
Daniel L Stephenson
1105 19th Ave SW
Minot ND 58701

N0IWD
James C Shanklin III
708 19th St NW
Minot ND 58701

KC0WSZ
Timothy W Langemo
816 1st Ave SW
Minot ND 58701

KC0HOQ
Matt A Black
2825 1st Ave SW
Minot ND 58701

KB0MMK
Daniel A Klingbeil
1120 1st NE
Minot ND 58703

KB0DSW
Thomas P Herrod
912 1st St NW
Minot ND 58701

KC0QFN
Jerome L Bakke
1731 1st St SE
Minot ND 58701

N0IKG
Thomas P Fraley
1301 1st St SW
Minot ND 58701

KF0ZV
James E Nagel
2524 2 Ave SW
Minot ND 587013334

KB8LXR
Gerald R Stevens
429 21st St NW
Minot ND 58703

KB0EDI
Rick D Fahrenbacher
706 22nd Ave NW
Minot ND 58703

W0EQP
Richard L Botton
204 22nd St NW
Minot ND 58701

KC0VDU
Jeffrey B Strange
413 23rd St NW
Minot ND 58703

K0CLD
Walter Mertz
620 24th Ave N west
Minot ND 58701

KA0SOM
Eunice A Mertz
620 24th Ave NW
Minot ND 58701

KB0DSY
Jesse L Griffin
625 25th Ave NW
Minot ND 58703

KC0JLV
Shane A Ziegler
209 25th St NW
Minot ND 58703

KF0IO
Larry B Henderson
303 25th St NW
Minot ND 58701

KB0SIN
Clifford J Hanson
1327 25th St SE
Minot ND 58701

K0SIN
Clifford J Hanson
1325 25th St SE 302
Minot ND 587015261

KE0PW
Karin S Will
912 26 Ave NW
Minot ND 58703

KC0YXC
Craig S Madsen
5730 27th Ave SE
Minot ND 58701

KA0SON
Janice M Klein
1325 27th St SE 209
Minot ND 587015210

W0HJU
Pius Klein
1325 27th St SE 209
Minot ND 587015210

N0TWY
Michael T Craw
1015 27th St SE 29
Minot ND 58701

KC0AQM
Eileen M Hanson
1325 27th St SE 302
Minot ND 587015261

KA0SOO
Crystal A Halseth
126 28th St SW
Minot ND 587013360

KC0NPT
Wesley J Halseth
126 28th St SW
Minot ND 587013360

W0GH
John F Valker
2519 2nd Ave SW
Minot ND 58701

KB0NCV
Leland L Larson
2524 2nd Ave SW
Minot ND 58701

KB0WWX
Shirley A Swensrud
2524 2nd SW
Minot ND 587020992

KF0DI
Robert E Dixon
500 30 Ave NW 15
Minot ND 58701

AB0KY
Robert E Dixon
500 30 Ave NW 15
Minot ND 58701

WF0M
James A Kaufer
500 32nd Ave SW Apt B
Minot ND 587017370

KB0BIM
Raymond E Folsom
909 38th St SE
Minot ND 58701

KB0BIN
Tammy S Folsom
909 38th St SE
Minot ND 58701

KD0HXX
Wayne E Johnson
823 3rd Ave NW
Minot ND 58703

N0ZWZ
Melvin J La Fontaine
1516 3rd Ave SE
Minot ND 58701

KF0IL
James A Fraley
826 3rd St SE
Minot ND 58701

KC0CU
Jackie D Fulton
1301 4 St SW
Minot ND 58701

WD0FQR
Vernon Allen Jr
920 41st St SE
Minot ND 58701

N7IV
Joseph M Ferrara
1057 45th Ave NE
Minot ND 58703

KB0CIZ
Peter M Hoffert
3410 47th St SE
Minot ND 58701

W0DEB
Deborah A Nelson
6940 4th Ave SW
Minot ND 58701

W0ND
Lynn A Nelson
6940 4th St SW
Minot ND 58701

W0CQ
Lynn A Nelson
6940 4th St SW
Minot ND 58701

KC0YAL
Rachel S Linnertz
604 4th St NE
Minot ND 587032510

KB0GVH
Florence G Braathen
5005 4th St SW
Minot ND 58701

KB0INN
Harlan L Braathen
5005 4th St SW
Minot ND 58701

K0MDF
Darel P Harrington
5009 4th St SW
Minot ND 58701

KC0CIY
Mary M Harrington
5009 4th St SW
Minot ND 58701

K0LN
North Dakota Radio Association
6940 4th St SW
Minot ND 58701

AB8NX
Gary T Schroeder
1721 4th St SW Unit 3
Minot ND 58701

KC0WCJ
Donald J Andrews
1303 5 Ave NW
Minot ND 58703

KC0LCG
Luann M Roberts
5120 51 Ave SE
Minot ND 58701

N0PBK
Daniel R Roberts
5120 51st Ave SE
Minot ND 58701

KD0QDK
Benjamin J Clark
1801 57th St NW
Minot ND 58703

AC0LY
James L Hartung
5920 62nd St SW
Minot ND 58701

KW2E
James L Hartung
5920 62nd St SW
Minot ND 58701

N0UCQ
James L Hartung
5920 62nd St SW
Minot ND 58701

KC0DYV
Darrel L Wilkerson II
1000 65 St NW
Minot ND 58701

KC0EBF
Nickle L Wilkerson
1000 65th St NW
Minot ND 58701

KD0CGA
Travis B Tubbs
14 6th Ave NE
Minot ND 58703

KD0CGB
Denay C Tubbs
14 6th Ave NE
Minot ND 58703

AA0UO
Wayne C Peterson
1319 6th Ave SE
Minot ND 58701

N0FKR
Harold Olson
733 6th Ave SW
Minot ND 58701

KB0UQA
David M Fries
1 6th S W L
Minot ND 58701

K9LO
Ernest R Swanson
2420 6th St NW
Minot ND 587030712

W0UEB
Warren L Shook
1935 6th St SE Apt 27
Minot ND 587016724

N0JDP
Kirk A Borud
1531 6th St SW
Minot ND 58701

KG0YK
Russell L Edington
1200 7 Ave NW
Minot ND 58701

KA0DXC
Marvin E Mertz
9800 79th Ave S E
Minot ND 58701

W0HVA
Richard A Wengel
1221 7th Ave NE
Minot ND 58703

KC0UET
Magic City Dx Club
1210 7th Ave SW
Minot ND 58701

WB0EBZ
Donald H Boucher
527 7th St NE
Minot ND 58701

N0EYY
Robert S Lipe
317 7th St NW
Minot ND 58701

KC0NUW
Anthony J Anderson
1937 7th St NW
Minot ND 58703

KC0NPV
Robert J G Anderson
1937 7th St NW
Minot ND 58703

N0CKB
Lawrence W Lilliquist
2042 7th St NW
Minot ND 58703

W0NGN
Magic City Dx Club
1210 7th St SW
Minot ND 58701

W0NGN
Gladys L Ekblad
1210 7th St SW
Minot ND 58701

K0QQ
Arthur H Ekblad
1210 7th St SW
Minot ND 587015704

N0RYJ
Gene R Rogers
1430 7th St SW
Minot ND 58701

KC0UTM
Christopher G Lathrop
9211 84th Ave SE
Minot ND 58701

KC0HOO
William P Curry
2416 8th St NW
Minot ND 58703

N0UAH
Vicky K Stigen
415 9th Ave NE
Minot ND 58701

KB0EQH
Bruce A Whittemore
1724 9th St SW
Minot ND 58701

N0NZF
Kimberly K Whittemore
1724 9th St SW
Minot ND 58701

K0BAE
Ramon W Swenson
1833 9th St SW
Minot ND 58701

N0KRZ
Lisa A Mahowald
617 Arbor Ave
Minot ND 58701

KB0NCW
Donald J Crepps
1007 Arthur Ln
Minot ND 58701

KC0FYB
John R Kinkade
3507 Arthur Ln
Minot ND 58701

AB0KZ
John R Kinkade
3507 Arthur Ln
Minot ND 58701

KC0ISW
Jeffrey R Kinkade
3507 Arthur Ln
Minot ND 58701

KE0WG
William R Rust
Rr 4 Box 214
Minot ND 58701

KC0BDL
Marlyn R Eklund
Rr 6 Box 322
Minot ND 58703

KA0JOJ
Leo R Brilz
Route 4 Box 60
Minot ND 58701

N0RYB
Chrisanne R Nelson
3905 Buttercup Ln
Minot ND 58701

N0RYG
Barry D Davis
4105 Buttercup Ln
Minot ND 58701

KC0DYJ
Adam M Jones
3 Cortland Dr
Minot ND 58703

KC8NWV
Roy C Roggenbuck
6500 CR 12 W
Minot ND 58701

N0NWY
Kay Schilla
7731 CR 15 W
Minot ND 587038400

KD0CGC
Laurie H Fifield
2309 Cressent Drive
Minot ND 58703

WB0JGN
Kim C Hagen
9 Fairway Dr
Minot ND 58701

KC0WSY
Trent A Hagen
9 Fairway Drive
Minot ND 58701

W0NVK
Weston A Bell
602 Forest Rd
Minot ND 58701

W0FOB
Fred O Brooks
12 Glacial Court
Minot ND 58703

KI0JT
Fred O Brooks
12 Glacial Ct
Minot ND 58701

KC0LAH
Margaret A Brooks
12 Glacial Ct
Minot ND 58703

W0PAB
Margaret A Brooks
12 Glacial Ct
Minot ND 58703

KA0DQX
Carlyle L Roth
1511 Glacial Dr
Minot ND 58701

KC0UZO
Ryan W Brown
1533 Hiawatha St SE
Minot ND 58701

KB0OZJ
Cecil L Corrigan
400 Hillcrest Dr
Minot ND 58701

KB0RVD
Charles L Moody
7950 Hwy 2 E Lot 128
Minot ND 58701

WA0GTU
Kermit S Mostad
6000 Hwy 52 S
Minot ND 58701

W0LNA
Robert W Brown
2025 Ida Mae Ct
Minot ND 58703

KB0ETD
Joyce E Flowers
81 Palmers Tr Ct
Minot ND 58701

W0PRN
Norris F Wissler
625-15Th St Se 62 Parkview Mhc
Minot ND 587014987

K0ROB
Robert S Lewis III
1940 S Broadway 312
Minot ND 58701

KB0RVR
Judson E Stone
2604 Skyline Dr
Minot ND 58703

KB0BP
John D Mc Cann
1234 Valley View Dr
Minot ND 58703

K0HFK
William Bossert
2101 W Central Ave
Minot ND 58701

W0QNW
Virgil N Nordstrom
817 W Central Ave
Minot ND 58701

WD0BCI
Todd R Enders
Minot ND 58702

AG0T
Todd R Enders
Minot ND 587020449

---

**FCC Amateur Radio Licenses in Minot AFB**

---

KC0GFX
Erin L Robinson
131 4 Sirocco Dr
Minot AFB ND 58704

KB0BIT
Elaine M Frankhouser
119-2 Coral Ct

Minot AFB ND 58704

KB0BIP
Neal A Clinehens
141-1 Delta Dr
Minot AFB ND 58704

KB3QPG
Nathaniel C Melzer
180 Delta Drive Apt 2
Minot AFB ND 58704

KB0ETJ
Edward M Wooten Jr
45-2 Dundee Dr
Minot AFB ND 58704

KA5WCT
Scott E Melia
105-1 Gramercy Ct
Minot AFB ND 58704

KB0BIQ
Kenneth R Asnes
103B Largo Ln
Minot AFB ND 58704

N0ZEP
James K King
117 Roaming Rd Apt 2
Minot AFB ND 58704

KC0EFO
Connie S Ronnie
102-2 Tangley Rd
Minot AFB ND 58704

KC0EFP
Mitchell S Ronnie
102-2 Tangley Rd
Minot AFB ND 58704

KC0IXX
Patrick T R Raynor
Dorm 222 Unit 94

Minot AFB ND 58704

KB0PMT
Robert A Smith
123-1 Winding Way
Minot AFB ND 58704

## FCC Amateur Radio Licenses in Minto

N0BMS
Clement B Houdek
341 Gillespie Ave
Minto ND 582610196

N0QLQ
Mark A Davis
PO Box 253
Minto ND 58261

## FCC Amateur Radio Licenses in Mohall

WD0CIU
Albert J Faulconbridge
404 Main St E
Mohall ND 587610458

WD0BEA
Marvin A Baska
Mohall ND 58761

## FCC Amateur Radio Licenses in Mott

KB0JIW
Carole A Woiwode
Route 1 Box 57
Mott ND 58646

KB0JIV
Joseph W T Woiwode
Rt 1 Box 57
Mott ND 58646

KD0JTL

Herbert E Quamme
407 Illinois Ave
Mott ND 58646

AC0WB
Herbert E Quamme
407 Illinois Ave
Mott ND 58646

## FCC Amateur Radio Licenses in Mountain

K0IDX
Ronald G Brown
12591 88th St NE
Mountain ND 58262

WA2EKW
Ronald G Brown
12591 88th St NE
Mountain ND 58262

## FCC Amateur Radio Licenses in Munich

KC0MO
Norbert O Rupp
10 Ryan
Munich ND 58352

W0NVV
Helen M Rupp
10 Ryan
Munich ND 58352

## FCC Amateur Radio Licenses in Napoleon

KC0OAL
Jerrilynn M Peterson
416 Ave B W
Napoleon ND 58561

AB0WU
Robert L Peterson

416 Ave B W
Napoleon ND 58561

WB0OFF
Howard E Holsti
Box 373
Napoleon ND 58561

KA0QWI
Clifford G Johnson
519 E Ave A
Napoleon ND 585617228

KA0VZA
Ellen H Johnson
Box 136 RR
Napoleon ND 58561

N0MPU
John J Kuntz
RR 110
Napoleon ND 58561

## FCC Amateur Radio Licenses in New England

KA0DQA
George G Bender Jr
309 E 8th Ave
New England ND 58647

## FCC Amateur Radio Licenses in New Leipzig

KC0VLA
Joshua A Amundson
317 4th Ave E
New Leipzig ND 58562

## FCC Amateur Radio Licenses in New Rockford

K0QPS
Fred H Wipperling
530 1st Ave S

New Rockford ND 583561607

N0RYA
Darlyne E Storwold
620 3rd Ave S
New Rockford ND 58356

WA7UEA
Donald P Storwold Sr
620 3rd Ave S
New Rockford ND 583561629

KG7ET
Ronald J Helliwell
807 4th Ave N
New Rockford ND 58356

KC0AJT
Richard J Steinbeck
Rr 1 Box 108
New Rockford ND 58356

KC0DUZ
Timothy C Hager
320 Central Ave
New Rockford ND 58356

KA7RKV
Daryl G Snyder
New Rockford ND 583560045

## FCC Amateur Radio Licenses in New Salem

W0WV
David A Holle
4710 34th St
New Salem ND 585639216

N0AQ
Neill J Holle
4710 34th St
New Salem ND 58563

N0III

Charles M Hendrickson
3885 40th St
New Salem ND 58563

KV0C
Jeff A Sloven
3770 CR 139
New Salem ND 58563

KD0OCO
Michael J Sloven
3770 CR 139
New Salem ND 58563

KD0REU
Mary J Sloven
3770 CR 139
New Salem ND 58563

KF0KG
Delbert C Bumann
307 Lake St
New Salem ND 58563

N0KSA
Corrie L Bumann
307 Lake St
New Salem ND 58563

W0OOD
William F Gaebe
116 N 8th St
New Salem ND 58563

## FCC Amateur Radio Licenses in New Town

K0CQQ
Arthur V Langved
4595 92nd Ave NW
New Town ND 58763

KC0JPO
John D Murphy Jr
New Town ND 58763

## FCC Amateur Radio Licenses in Newburg

W0IDI
Quentin J Falkenbury
2016 3rd Ave
Newburg ND 58762

KC2CIM
Quentin J Falkenbury
2016 3rd Ave
Newburg ND 58762

ND0CW
David M Heintzleman
228 Akin St
Newburg ND 58762

KD0MSC
Northern Tier Ssb Club
228 Akin St
Newburg ND 58762

ND0SB
Northern Tier Ssb Club
228 Akin St
Newburg ND 58762

K8BBM
David M Heintzleman
228 Akin St
Newburg ND 58762

W7EZI
Edward L Weigel
462 W Main St
Newburg ND 58762

## FCC Amateur Radio Licenses in Niagara

KC0CRT
Tena K O Neill
403 Ransom Ave

Niagara ND 58266

N0WWL
Thomas E O Neill
403 Ransom Ave
Niagara ND 58266

KE0T
Thomas E O'Neill
403 Ransom Ave
Niagara ND 58266

## FCC Amateur Radio Licenses in Ninot

KC0HOP
Lucas J Niess
10800 86 St SE
Ninot ND 58701

## FCC Amateur Radio Licenses in Noonan

KE6VXK
Jerome W Walter
401 S Main St
Noonan ND 587650103

KB0LQX
Anne M Meisel
Noonan ND 58765

N7KWX
Lester L Sampson
Noonan ND 58765

## FCC Amateur Radio Licenses in Northwood

KB0OGU
Raymond A Nemoseck Jr
3804 10th Ave NE
Northwood ND 58267

KD0PSB

Edward A Bina
470 34th St NE
Northwood ND 58267

KC0SD
Norman G Bakken
RR II Box 152
Northwood ND 58267

KA0IOD
Charles W Ostlie
Northwood ND 58267

## FCC Amateur Radio Licenses in Oakes

N0NDX
James D Ptacek
11340 81st St SE
Oakes ND 58474

KA0UIH
Charles K Ptacek
1014 E Main Ave
Oakes ND 58474

KD0OUB
Steven K Thompson
8596 Happy Acres
Oakes ND 58474

KA0PKK
James D Ptacek
16 N 12th St
Oakes ND 58474

## FCC Amateur Radio Licenses in Oberon

WD0HOQ
David L Donaldson
6454 Highway 281
Oberon ND 583579603

N0PCX

Steven B Cartier
6673 Hwy 281
Oberon ND 583579691

## FCC Amateur Radio Licenses in Oriska

N0SCP
T R Trautmann
607 2nd Ave
Oriska ND 58063

KI0FH
Raymond M Triebold
12205 32nd St SE
Oriska ND 58063

KB0RTR
Anthony J Yanish
510 9th Ave
Oriska ND 580634116

KB0SII
Sebastian E Ertelt
RR 1
Oriska ND 58063

KB0KFU
Larry K Bietz
Oriska ND 58063

## FCC Amateur Radio Licenses in Page

KC0NDB
Anna K Vosgerau
1926 128th Ave SE
Page ND 58064

## FCC Amateur Radio Licenses in Park River

W0OJS
Duane L Gustafson
107 Kensington
Park River ND 58270

WB0ITD
David J Praska
208 Sumit Ave
Park River ND 58270

W0DJP
Praskas Amateur Radio Club
208 Summit Ave S
Park River ND 58270

KC0KUO
Jeffrey J Dieter
705 Wadge Ave
Park River ND 58270

W0JJD
Jeffrey J Dieter
705 Wadge Ave S
Park River ND 58270

N0JVZ
Kevin H Knutson
Park River ND 58270

KA0FDR
Guy G Praska
Park River ND 58270

## FCC Amateur Radio Licenses in Parshall

KD0KMA
Carolyn L Folden
Parshall ND 58770

## FCC Amateur Radio Licenses in Pembina

KB0ZWL
Jennifer J Horning
PO Box 165
Pembina ND 58271

N0XVZ

Stephen W Horning
PO Box 165
Pembina ND 58271

## FCC Amateur Radio Licenses in Penn

KA0KXI
Warren L Parsons
6860 54th St NE
Penn ND 58362

## FCC Amateur Radio Licenses in Perth

N0NTU
Paul Juntunen
9641 57th Ave NE
Perth ND 583639692

## FCC Amateur Radio Licenses in Pisek

KK0MG
Robert E Lewis
6152 CR 12A
Pisek ND 58273

KK7MG
Robert E Lewis
6152 CR 12A
Pisek ND 582730058

## FCC Amateur Radio Licenses in Portal

W0BHT
Edmund D Mc Ginnis Jr
Box 186
Portal ND 58772

## FCC Amateur Radio Licenses in Portland

KE0XT
Robert L Aasen

14673 1st St NE
Portland ND 582749441

NJ0B
Howard K Seaver
816 8th St
Portland ND 58274

KE0DM
Gerald B Tollefson
816 8th St
Portland ND 58274

WA0OIZ
Lauren A Erickson
Rr 1 Box 129
Portland ND 58274

KA0ZKK
Surges L Vinje
1 RR 1
Portland ND 58274

## FCC Amateur Radio Licenses in Powers Lake

AB0CR
Denny B Ramsdell
Box 222
Powers Lake ND 58773

W0WWZ
Edward P Moriarty
Powers Lake ND 58773

## FCC Amateur Radio Licenses in Ray

KB0WEH
Jerry W Hauge
11151 58th St NW
Ray ND 58849

KB0WEI
Christine L Hauge
11151 58th St NW

Ray ND 58849

WD0GMD
Bernard L Arcand
Ray ND 588490523

## FCC Amateur Radio Licenses in Regan

KB0QZI
Dennis M Olson
Regan ND 58477

## FCC Amateur Radio Licenses in Regent

K0LU
Leon J Kirschemann
11024 73St SW
Regent ND 58650

WA0NZO
Leon J Kirschemann
Hcr 2 Box 21
Regent ND 58650

KB0NBZ
Ardmore Quamme
85 Main Ave Box 202
Regent ND 58650

KG0AU
Curtis R Olson
Regent ND 58650

## FCC Amateur Radio Licenses in Reynolds

KA0PAB
Dwight W Ollman
221 22nd St NE
Reynolds ND 58275

## FCC Amateur Radio Licenses in Rhame

KB0CDT
Helen J Edwards
305 Main
Rhame ND 586510013

KC0ADL
Henry O Waller
107 W 1st St
Rhame ND 58651

N0KQO
Ronald E Eagon
Rhame ND 58651

## FCC Amateur Radio Licenses in Richardton

K0RFS
Ray F Sitter
8869 23rd St SW
Richardton ND 58652

KC0DDL
Ray F Sitter
8869 23rd St SW
Richardton ND 58652

N0HUR
John R Elkins
9074 42 St SW
Richardton ND 58652

WA0SVZ
John D Seiler
Assumption Abbey
Richardton ND 58652

WA0UQD
Odo M Muggli
Assumption Abbey
Richardton ND 586520901

W0BHF
Charles W Alpert
127 D St N Apt D
Richardton ND 58652

KA0SXU
Les Alpert
Richardton ND 58652

WB7QZD
Anthony R Aman
Richardton ND 58652

## FCC Amateur Radio Licenses in Riverdale

KB8CL
Gary L Blankenship
Riverdale ND 585650521

## FCC Amateur Radio Licenses in Robinson

KD0NAM
Matthew A Bon
2350 31st Ave SE
Robinson ND 58478

## FCC Amateur Radio Licenses in Rock Lake

N0IWS
Roger J Kurtti
9561 61st Ave NE
Rock Lake ND 58365

N0OJS
Mertie K Kurtti
9653 61st Ave NE
Rock Lake ND 58365

WC0M
Roger W Kurtti
9651 61st Ave NE
Rock Lake ND 58365

N0GUV
Erling A Kurtti
Box 34
Rock Lake ND 58365

## FCC Amateur Radio Licenses in Rogers

KC0PAF
Kenneth M Jewett
Rogers ND 58479

N0KMJ
Kenneth M Jewett
Rogers ND 58479

## FCC Amateur Radio Licenses in Rolette

KD0NTK
Luther A Stave
3063 82nd St
Rolette ND 58366

N0WND
Luther A Stave
3063 82nd St
Rolette ND 58366

W0GIN
Luther A Stave
3063 82nd St
Rolette ND 58366

KA0QVR
Kenneth W Tastad
Rr 1 Box 130
Rolette ND 58366

## FCC Amateur Radio Licenses in Rolla

KB8RO
Daniel L Dildine
Rolla ND 58367

KB0QYV
Du Wayne K Hoffman
Rolla ND 583670206

---

**FCC Amateur Radio Licenses in Rugby**

---

N0IJR
Thomas J Childress
315 2nd Ave SE
Rugby ND 58368

WB0ATJ
William T Bosley
329 2nd St SW
Rugby ND 58368

KC0FTI
Richard D Voeller
808 4th Ave SW
Rugby ND 58368

KA0QDB
Dennis K Miller
2869 64th St NE
Rugby ND 58368

WB0BMG
Leona E Kjelstrom
124 9th St E
Rugby ND 58368

WB0BMH
Edwin J Kjelstrom
124 9th St SE
Rugby ND 58368

KD0FNS
Lyle W Ramsey
601 Highway 2 SW
Rugby ND 583682602

N0HIC
Karlyle A Erickson

3640 Hwy 2 E
Rugby ND 583687637

KB0BZQ
Harvey D Piper
800 S Main Ave
Rugby ND 583682118

N0GUY
Mark A Krogstad
301 SW 2nd St
Rugby ND 58368

---

**FCC Amateur Radio Licenses in Ruso**

---

WA0CHR
Roy W Willoughby
Rte 1 Box 46
Ruso ND 58778

WA0OOG
Bruce A Lorenz
1 Flower St
Ruso ND 587787803

---

**FCC Amateur Radio Licenses in Ruthville**

---

KA0AHZ
Mary L Bradley
99 Palmers Mhp
Ruthville ND 58701

---

**FCC Amateur Radio Licenses in Ryder**

---

N0ZWY
Beau J Simmons
Box 82
Ryder ND 58779

N0RDD
Dean G Simmons
Ryder ND 58779

## FCC Amateur Radio Licenses in Saint Michael

KF0IY
Morlin L Madson
Rr 2 Box 59
Saint Michael ND 58370

## FCC Amateur Radio Licenses in Saint Thomas

KA9QJB
Richard L Lunde
Saint Thomas ND 58276

N0SCQ
Ronald G Berg
Saint Thomas ND 58276

## FCC Amateur Radio Licenses in Sawyer

N0TKG
Paul L Meisel
22500 42nd St SE
Sawyer ND 58781

K0AJW
Minot Amateur Radio Association
22500 42nd St SE
Sawyer ND 58781

AB0NT
Scott D Pfenning
12500 90th St E
Sawyer ND 58781

## FCC Amateur Radio Licenses in Scranton

WD0DAF
Denis O Hansey
Box 106
Scranton ND 58653

KB0CFZ
John W Moor
Rt 1 Box 221
Scranton ND 58653

N0JSY
Dale H Freymiller
Rr 1 Box 40
Scranton ND 58653

## FCC Amateur Radio Licenses in Selfridge

KA0SXS
Deborah L Vollmuth
Selfridge ND 58568

## FCC Amateur Radio Licenses in Sheldon

K0BWH
Robert A Buss
5678 140th Ave SE
Sheldon ND 58068

K0HQP
Linda G Buss
5678 140th Ave SE
Sheldon ND 58068

W0RLE
Don G Mc Dougall
14548 58th St SE
Sheldon ND 58068

## FCC Amateur Radio Licenses in Sherwood

KC0BDM
Scott I Rostad
132 3rd Ave E
Sherwood ND 58782

N0TKH

Dori L Aho
Sherwood ND 587820046

## FCC Amateur Radio Licenses in Sheyenne

WB0UPT
Lynn E Erickson
6739 31st NE
Sheyenne ND 58374

KB0VUJ
Marvin Madson
Box 227
Sheyenne ND 58374

KD7TV
Clarence T Erickson
Sheyenne ND 58374

## FCC Amateur Radio Licenses in Sibley

K0AAJ
Don A Ven Huizen
139 Lake Ave
Sibley ND 58429

## FCC Amateur Radio Licenses in Solen

KD0ATX
Charles M Stevens
2845 CR 135
Solen ND 58570

## FCC Amateur Radio Licenses in Souris

W0FNZ
Milo A Shelton
Rr 2 Box 52
Souris ND 58783

## FCC Amateur Radio Licenses in South Heart

KC0HSS
Kenneth D Kudrna
11961 41st St SW
South Heart ND 58655

## FCC Amateur Radio Licenses in Stanley

KB0FKT
Joseph A Aho
306 6 Ave SE
Stanley ND 58784

KB0FJM
Patricia A Aho
Box 172
Stanley ND 58784

KB0WVQ
Kevin L Olson
5995 Hwy 8  Endanders
Stanley ND 58784

KB0WVR
Robin E Olson
5995 Hwy 8 Enanders
Stanley ND 58784

KC0DYX
Dennis A Beehler
915 S Main St
Stanley ND 587840461

KB0CIR
James E Aho
Stanley ND 58784

KC0BET
Lyle D Aho
Stanley ND 58384

K0GGH

John O Enander
Stanley ND 58784

KC0QJG
Kristal L Aho
Stanley ND 587840172

KC0BET
Kristal L Aho
Stanley ND 587840172

KB0YGP
Prairie Hills Repeater Association
Stanley ND 587840172

## FCC Amateur Radio Licenses in Starweather

KB0YBO
Ginger L Thacker
Starweather ND 583770027

## FCC Amateur Radio Licenses in Sterling

KD0EFP
Craig C Bohlander
104 Linda Ave
Sterling ND 58572

## FCC Amateur Radio Licenses in Strasburg

K0JIM
James M Hanson
405 1st St S
Strasburg ND 58573

N0FWD
Michael J Hanson
405 1st St S
Strasburg ND 58573

## FCC Amateur Radio Licenses in Streeter

WA0FEU
Paul E Nyren
4647 47th Ave SE
Streeter ND 58483

## FCC Amateur Radio Licenses in Surrey

KB5NJF
Paul Chaplar
5500 111th St NE
Surrey ND 58785

WB0TJL
Robert A Feller
Box 157
Surrey ND 58785

KD0VT
Diane I Vitko
Surrey ND 58785

KD0VS
Mitchell A Vitko
Surrey ND 58785

## FCC Amateur Radio Licenses in Sykeston

KC0RZN
Todd P Hafner
343 49th Ave NE
Sykeston ND 58486

## FCC Amateur Radio Licenses in Thompson

KC0OMY
Wayne K Riveland
1346 10th Ave NE
Thompson ND 58278

KC0CFR
Joseph J Simon
402 3rd St Box 303
Thompson ND 58278

KC0GWL
Thomas G Corwin
326 5th St
Thompson ND 58278

KB0LXZ
Susan L Hahn
9 Goodwin Ave
Thompson ND 58278

KB0LYA
Bryan C Hahn
9 Goodwin Ave
Thompson ND 58278

KC0YXB
Nancy M Yoshida
1079 Harvest Ln NE
Thompson ND 58278

K9DIG
Nancy M Yoshida
1079 Harvest Ln NE
Thompson ND 58278

KD0LZJ
Greater Grand Forks Schools Amateur
Radio Club
1079 Harvest Ln NE
Thompson ND 58278

N0GFK
Greater Grand Forks Schools Amateur
Radio Club
1079 Harvest Ln NE
Thompson ND 58278

**FCC Amateur Radio Licenses in
Tolna**

KC0AEY
Duane M Rude
2799 96th Ave NE
Tolna ND 583809546

N0VKH
Valerie G Johnson
Box 145
Tolna ND 58380

N0WKA
Clifford H Gleason
Box 185
Tolna ND 58380

KC0AEZ
Randal S Waldo
Rr 1 Box 90
Tolna ND 583809529

KC0AFA
Melane E Waldo
Rr 1 Box 90
Tolna ND 583809529

KA0SLF
Robert D Gleason
2842 Gleason Dr
Tolna ND 583809599

KD0CSA
Rodney S Stoa
707 Minnesota Ave
Tower City ND 580714220

**FCC Amateur Radio Licenses in
Towner**

KD0AKX
Stanley E Beck
460 78th St N
Towner ND 58788

## FCC Amateur Radio Licenses in Turtle Lake

KD0RMF
Richard A Anderson
Turtle Lake ND 58575

KI0JG
Bruce A Kocher
Turtle Lake ND 58575

## FCC Amateur Radio Licenses in Valley City

KC0GBX
Maurice W Wick
3250 117th Ave SE
Valley City ND 58072

KB0RLS
Rodli J Pederson
120 14th St NW
Valley City ND 58072

N0KTL
James F Anderson
455 2nd St NE
Valley City ND 58072

N0KGE
Dale E Stanford
11819 31st St SE
Valley City ND 58072

N0KMN
Lori D Stanford
11819 31st St SE
Valley City ND 58072

N0LSF
Nadine G Van Dyke
11033 33 St SE
Valley City ND 58072

W0BTW

Gregory J Lewis
11415 33rd St SE
Valley City ND 58072

N0LSY
Jim J Van Dyke
11033 33rd St SE
Valley City ND 58072

KA0CRJ
Catherine D Dawkins
746 4th Ave NW Box 395
Valley City ND 58072

W0YEQ
James G Lade
425 4th St SW
Valley City ND 580723920

W0YEQ
Judith A Stahl
468 5th St NW
Valley City ND 58072

WA0HBE
Judith A Stahl
468 5th St NW
Valley City ND 58072

W0JDH
Vitres P Ficek
327 6th St NW
Valley City ND 58072

KB0EKF
Jeremy T Van Dyke
Rr 3 Box 105
Valley City ND 58072

K8IMV
Lowell J Busching
Box 451
Valley City ND 580720451

W0SRH

Vernon J Monson
979 Central Ave N
Valley City ND 58072

KC0RYC
William A Duppler
4605 CR 21
Valley City ND 58072

KA0VWS
Robert T Hefty
481 Viking Dr
Valley City ND 58072

KB0VSX
Wade T Stine
1135 Viking Dr 77
Valley City ND 58072

## FCC Amateur Radio Licenses in Velva

W0PUP
Russell W Burgess
Rt 1 Box 219
Velva ND 58790

## FCC Amateur Radio Licenses in Wahpeton

WB0FMM
Ella A Oscarson
6965 174th Ave SE
Wahpeton ND 58075

W0END
Three Rivers Amateur Radio Club
8315 180 Ave SE
Wahpeton ND 58075

KD0OUD
Adam J Mortenson
8315 180 Ave SE
Wahpeton ND 58075

N0UET
Brian K Mortenson
8315 180 Ave SE
Wahpeton ND 58075

WB0GAH
Three Rivers Amateur Radio Club
8315 180 Ave SE
Wahpeton ND 58075

KC0YCP
John T Mortenson
8315 180th Ave SE
Wahpeton ND 58075

K0UET
John T Mortenson
8315 180th Ave SE
Wahpeton ND 58075

KD0OUA
Matthew J Mortenson
8315 180th Ave SE
Wahpeton ND 58075

WB0GFY
Larry D Drake
77 4th Ave N
Wahpeton ND 580753940

K0MSS
Theresa J Vaagen
424 4th St S
Wahpeton ND 58075

KC0GQG
Theresa J Vaagen
424 4th St S
Wahpeton ND 58075

N0MSS
Ross C Vaagen
424 4th St S
Wahpeton ND 58075

AA7RY
Steven J Thiel
85 5th Ave S
Wahpeton ND 58075

AB5ZI
Lynn D Drewianka
307 5th St N Apt 4
Wahpeton ND 58075

KD0NZV
Robert M Aho
307 5th St N Apt 4
Wahpeton ND 58075

WA0RWK
Jeanie M Hoff
17475 66th St SE
Wahpeton ND 58075

N0SRR
Bruce A Woytassek
428 7th St N
Wahpeton ND 58075

K0SEB
Robert E Olson
17580 85th St SE
Wahpeton ND 58075

KC0ACE
Brian L Mc Waters
919 8th Ave N
Wahpeton ND 580754943

KI0GY
Mark A Spiekermeier
1506 Ave B
Wahpeton ND 58075

KA0LPH
Joseph Flaa
Rt 1 Box 77B
Wahpeton ND 50875

KB0BWK
Kerwin J Pankratz
College Complex SE 307
Wahpeton ND 58075

K0GGL
Joseph W Thane
17850 CR 10
Wahpeton ND 58075

KB0MHL
Ronald R Matthys
18270 CR 16
Wahpeton ND 58075

WB0SHC
Lowell F Johnson
1640 N 5th St
Wahpeton ND 58075

KB0BSO
James M Viele
428 N 6th St
Wahpeton ND 58075

WT0S
Donald J Viele
428 N 6th St
Wahpeton ND 58075

KD0OUC
Darin M Carlsrud
911 Western Rd Apt 9
Wahpeton ND 58075

WB0YOT
Rick A Hendrickson
1414 Westmore Ave
Wahpeton ND 58075

## FCC Amateur Radio Licenses in Walhalla

W0SDN
Everette L Bailly

500 4th St Apt 11
Walhalla ND 58282

K0ABC
Doyle E Tongen
611 Central Ave
Walhalla ND 58282

N6OXX
Geoffrey M Avery
612 Central Ave
Walhalla ND 58282

KA0PZD
Erwin H Letkeman
Box 473 Hwy 32 S
Walhalla ND 58282

KA0YAE
Frederick H Allen III
803 Mountain Ave
Walhalla ND 58282

KC0HGH
Jeffrey D Amoth
1007 Riverside
Walhalla ND 58282

W0IAS
Robert W Meece
Walhalla ND 58282

## FCC Amateur Radio Licenses in Washburn

KD0QLA
Jerry L Thompson
602 4th Ave
Washburn ND 58577

KC0AFB
Chad A Dahme
1227 Chestnut Drive
Washburn ND 58577

## FCC Amateur Radio Licenses in Watford City

KB0RRY
Donald A Forland
Rr 1 Box 9
Watford City ND 58854

N0HYQ
Vonne H Tarnavsky
12771 Long X Rd
Watford City ND 58854

KB0QIW
Jennifer R Metzgar
Watford City ND 58854

W0PKY
Fred R Piper
Watford City ND 588540646

## FCC Amateur Radio Licenses in West Fargo

KA0EFB
Eugene W Orson
314 10 1/2 Ave E
West Fargo ND 580783032

KD0RKR
Delbert K Jennings
314 10th Ave E
West Fargo ND 58078

K0BOB
John A Gjerdevig
507 10th Ave E
West Fargo ND 58078

N0YPF
Michael L Kjar
237 10th Ave W
West Fargo ND 58078

W0ATF

Theodore S Clennon
901 10th Ave W Apt 15
West Fargo ND 58078

KB0ZAF
Natalie J Koch
1401 12 St E 7
West Fargo ND 58078

KD0YX
Timothy L Gooding
421 12th Ave E
West Fargo ND 58078

N0XSB
James F Baltezore
1424 12th St Ct
West Fargo ND 58078

N0ZQE
Joan M Baltezore
1424 12th St Ct
West Fargo ND 58078

N0AHD
Frank J Hoffman Jr
114 15th Ave E
West Fargo ND 58078

KC0MOZ
Ryan W Odonnell
880 16 Ave W
West Fargo ND 58078

KB0UYY
Lee P Sveinson
1425 16th Ave E
West Fargo ND 58078

KC0OHA
Heather M Goebel
225 17 1/2 St E
West Fargo ND 58078

AC0BT

Dennis L Lokken
724 18th Ave W
West Fargo ND 58078

KD0HPC
Jeffrey W Cheney
502 1st Ave NW
West Fargo ND 58078

KD0IEG
Norma J Andersen
621 20 1/2 Ave E
West Fargo ND 58078

K0NJA
Norma J Andersen
621 20 1/2 Ave E
West Fargo ND 58078

W0KWA
Kenneth W Andersen
631 20 1/2 Ave E
West Fargo ND 58078

W0MKA
Mathew K Andersen
631 20 1/2 Ave E
West Fargo ND 58078

KB0LFV
Mathew K Andersen
631 20 1/2 Ave E
West Fargo ND 58078

KG0ZU
Kenneth W Andersen
631 20 1/2 Ave E
West Fargo ND 58078

N0VHB
Jeffrey D Goebel
632 21st St E
West Fargo ND 58078

KC0LOM

David C Hillerson
435 22 St E Apt L
West Fargo ND 58078

KC0VMZ
Joey P Trelstad
422 22nd St E
West Fargo ND 58078

WB0DSF
Robert M Kirkeby
122 2nd Ave E
West Fargo ND 58078

KB0QZD
Glenn D Ellingsberg
1225 2nd St W
West Fargo ND 580782616

W0MMZ
David M Beasley
1142 39 1/2 Ave W
West Fargo ND 58078

KC0VKX
Charles W Dosh
121 3rd Ave E
West Fargo ND 58078

KC0VOO
Shawn A Burckhard
2025 3rd Ave E
West Fargo ND 58078

KD0LUW
Matthew W Nelson
1529 3rd St W
West Fargo ND 58078

KB0NDK
James A Bird
117 4th Ave E
West Fargo ND 58078

KC0DZB

Bruce R Steele
431 4th Ave E 611
West Fargo ND 58078

KC0JBQ
Andrew J Steele
425 4th Ave E 514
West Fargo ND 580781951

WB0NFX
John P Steiner
508 4th Ave NW
West Fargo ND 58078

KC0KBN
April R Goble
402 5th Ave E Apt 104
West Fargo ND 58078

KC0AFW
Lucius M Bennett
608 5th St Ct
West Fargo ND 58078

KD0NQZ
Kellen D Perry
3538 5th St W
West Fargo ND 58078

W0VET
Bruce R Steele
306 6th Ave E
West Fargo ND 58078

N0XHE
Rob V Becherl
118 6th Ave W
West Fargo ND 58078

KC0FHD
Timothy J Olson
517 6th St E Apt 1
West Fargo ND 580782825

KB0WFS

Brian K Frank
430 6th St E 136
West Fargo ND 58078

N0SDD
Kevin M Rezac
307 6th St W
West Fargo ND 58078

KD0PKT
Darren D Honrud
2943 7St W 108
West Fargo ND 58078

WA0LIA
Lance K Lee
301 7th Ave E
West Fargo ND 58078

N0LMU
David L Mjolsness
443 7th Ave E
West Fargo ND 58078

N0WQZ
David A Lund
639 7th Ave W
West Fargo ND 58078

KC0LON
Crystal D Seelhammer
639 7th Ave W
West Fargo ND 58078

KB0WFU
Jonathan S Pringle
725 7th Ave W
West Fargo ND 58078

N0WQY
Adam D Lund
639 7th Ave W
West Fargo ND 58078

KC0AEJ

Marie C Lund
639 7th Ave W
West Fargo ND 58078

N0SDE
James A Kirchen
819 7th St E
West Fargo ND 58078

KC0LOJ
Meghan M Kirchen
819 7th St E
West Fargo ND 58078

WB0AEM
Douglas L Jenson
608 8th Ave E
West Fargo ND 58078

N0SRY
Donald A Van Cleve
1427 8th St
West Fargo ND 58078

WA3QQF
Dale A Redmer
2703 9th St NW
West Fargo ND 580783903

KD0OLY
Brian E Roberts
1618 Birchwood Dr
West Fargo ND 58078

KC0QXH
Per F Jensen
330 Edgewater Dr
West Fargo ND 58078

KC0RSB
Luke F Jensen
330 Edgewater Dr
West Fargo ND 58078

WA0EAX

Roger J Klocke Sr
750 Elm St
West Fargo ND 58078

KB0VSV
Cheri L Verdoorn
109 Francis St
West Fargo ND 58078

K0DVV
David W Verdoorn Jr
109 Francis St
West Fargo ND 58078

KR0V
David W Verdoorn Jr
109 Francis St
West Fargo ND 58078

KB0DV
David W Verdoorn Jr
109 Francis St
West Fargo ND 58078

W0DV
David W Verdoorn Jr
109 Francis St
West Fargo ND 58078

KB0PTV
David W Verdoorn Jr
109 Francis St
West Fargo ND 58078

KC0CQI
Eric M Wiinanen
894 Homestead Ct
West Fargo ND 58078

KC0UEQ
Sheldon Fettig
1844 Huntington Ln
West Fargo ND 58078

KC0SHQ

Madelyn R Kitzan
3305 Meadow Way
West Fargo ND 58078

KC0SHR
Rodney R Kitzan
3305 Meadow Way
West Fargo ND 58078

WA0MJF
Robert J Jenks
1106 Parkway Dr
West Fargo ND 580787753

KC0BDS
Christopher J Ebens
1068 Parkway Ln
West Fargo ND 58078

N0FDR
Curtis J Malafa
671 Pleasant Run
West Fargo ND 58078

KA0RWX
Chris A Stangeland
3850 Willow Rd
West Fargo ND 58078

WA0FDV
John A Stangeland
3850 Willow Rd
West Fargo ND 58078

KC0TEO
Steve M Parsons
West Fargo ND 58078

KB0WFV
Gina M Becherl
West Fargo ND 58078

WA0TXD
Sherman E Waagen
West Fargo ND 580780514

## FCC Amateur Radio Licenses in Westhope

KB0DDE
Bobby J Beaudrie
Westhope ND 58793

## FCC Amateur Radio Licenses in Williston

KC0CMV
David J Erickson
505 10th Ave W
Williston ND 58801

KC0JBK
Michael T Gerszewski
5029 132nd Trl NW
Williston ND 58801

KB0NAX
Madge A Meisel
3804 13th Ave E
Williston ND 58801

KB0KEC
George A Meisel
3804 13th Ave E
Williston ND 588016803

KC0PHX
James J Assid Jr
923 13th Ave W
Williston ND 58801

KC0HOF
Marc D Russell
1007 13th Ave W Apt
Williston ND 58801

KA4WHE
Jerry E Love
5008 143rd Ave NW
Williston ND 58801

KB0RRZ
Eugene M Jorgenson
5819 145th Ave NW
Williston ND 58801

AB0JX
Eugene M Jorgenson
5819 145th Ave NW
Williston ND 58801

KB0LIP
Teina M Nunberg
4237 147th Ave NW
Williston ND 58801

KB0LIQ
Ryan J Aune
4237 147th Ave NW
Williston ND 58801

KB0LIR
Derek L Aune
4237 147th Ave NW
Williston ND 58801

KB0PUR
Jason F Aune
4237 147th Ave NW
Williston ND 58801

N0WJO
Dwight E Aune
4237 147th Ave NW
Williston ND 58801

N0XBX
Barbara J Aune
4237 147th Ave NW
Williston ND 58801

KC0APM
Amanda L Aune
4327 147th Ave NW
Williston ND 58801

KC7WWW
Shad D Pippin
102 14th St W Apt 16
Williston ND 58801

K0VOC
Oscar H Halvorson
906 16th Ave W
Williston ND 58801

KC0HUX
Darren L Reinholdt
2324 17th Ave W Apt 103
Williston ND 58801

WD0EYA
Henry N Marxen Jr
714 1st Ave E
Williston ND 588015408

KC0KEU
Connie J Thomson
516 1st Ave W
Williston ND 58801

WA5TLP
Virgil L Jiles Jr
309 22nd St
Williston ND 58801

KB0WEJ
Mitchell E Roth
1314 23rd St W
Williston ND 588013141

K0ITP
Bertha Swenson
1001 24th St W
Williston ND 58801

KE7ZCB
James C Mattson
1802 27th St W
Williston ND 58801

K0AYZ
David B Pederson
1409 2nd Ave E
Williston ND 58801

WD0APE
Earl R Gross
809 3 Ave E
Williston ND 58801

KA9ZFM
Patrick R Pfeiffer
1812 30th St W
Williston ND 58801

KC0MWP
William H Maisey
505 3rd Ave E
Williston ND 58801

AB0XD
Earl R Gross
809 3rd Ave E
Williston ND 58801

N7RSF
Richard S Fisher
828 3rd Ave W 6
Williston ND 58801

KB0MLX
Kenneth J Quamme
309 40th St E
Williston ND 58801

KB0RM
Thomas M Flath
612 4th Ave E
Williston ND 58801

KD7EZP
Jennifer L Dunker
308 4th Ave E
Williston ND 58801

KB0RSA
Phillip J Gunderson
823 4th St W
Williston ND 588014802

KC0CMT
Paul M Gunderson
823 4th St W
Williston ND 588014802

KC0PHV
Leslie R Heidner
13380 57th St NW Lot 126
Williston ND 58801

WD0EKD
Ronald J Mayer
1102 7th Ave E
Williston ND 58801

KC7HXA
Corey J Candee
2025 8th Ave E
Williston ND 58801

KC0UCJ
Matthew P Schlemper
522 8th Ave W
Williston ND 58801

KJ7TS
Charles E Lear
2220 9th Ave E
Williston ND 588016220

KB0PEF
Daniel P Eisele
Rt 1 Box 107W
Williston ND 58801

KB0TKW
Sherry L Heinrich
Rr 4 Box 197A Hwy 1804 E
Williston ND 58801

KC0CMS
Atrhur G Miller
Rr3 Box 263
Williston ND 588019416

KC0CMU
Vincent K Miller
Rr3 Box 263
Williston ND 588019416

KB0NEM
Ernest Sylte
208 E 20th St
Williston ND 58801

KC0UCI
George D Perry
321 E Broadway
Williston ND 58801

KA0UOX
Keith D Schmaltz
13427 Grandview Drive
Williston ND 58801

NF0S
Gary G Sundquist
1810 Sioux St
Williston ND 58801

KB0NAW
Gary D Wendel
2802 Skyway Ct
Williston ND 58801

WD0CCC
Timothy J Pederson
706 University Ave
Williston ND 58801

KC7AA
David A Brueni
2405 University Ave
Williston ND 58801

KC0HUW
James R Gunderson
823 W 4th St
Williston ND 58801

KB0LD
Bradley C Nelson
1502 W Broadway
Williston ND 58801

KC0PSE
Alvin J Jacobson
412 W 2nd St
Williston ND 58801

KC0CMW
Kenneth E Hiltner
710 W Broadway
Williston ND 58801

KC0PHW
Thomas C Rolfstad
Williston ND 58801

KC0KUH
Williston Basin Amateur Radio Club
Williston ND 58801

KC0PSF
Steven L Price
Williston ND 58802

KC0PSD
Thomas C Rolfstad Sr
Williston ND 588022016

K0WSN
Williston Basin Amateur Radio Club
Williston ND 588022048

**FCC Amateur Radio Licenses in
Willow City**

WA0HUD

Robert E Withey
302 Hwy 60 N
Willow City ND 583844013

W0HUD
Robert E Withey
302 Hwy 60 N
Willow City ND 583844013

**FCC Amateur Radio Licenses in
Wilton**

KC0MNP
Lance M Holden
600 331st Ave NW
Wilton ND 58579

KS0G
Mark C Mathys
114 5th St S
Wilton ND 58579

N0JJW
Cynthia J Mathys
114 5th St S
Wilton ND 58579

KC0OM
Andrew W Gregoryk
Wilton ND 58579

**FCC Amateur Radio Licenses in
Wimbledon**

W0WRW
Chester E Menz
Rr 2 Box 9
Wimbledon ND 58492

**FCC Amateur Radio Licenses in
Wishek**

WA6HRE
John W Coddington
Wishek ND 584950572

## FCC Amateur Radio Licenses in Wolford

N0GCE
Cleo A Yoder
7620 48th Ave NE
Wolford ND 58385

KB0NGB
Myron D Kauffman
Box 474
Wolford ND 58385

## FCC Amateur Radio Licenses in Wyndmere

KD0ACE
Bradley M Hofman
247 2nd St
Wyndmere ND 58081

WD0AFX
Russell L Janssen
First Gilead
Wyndmere ND 58081

K0TNI
John H Bailey
7850 Hwy 18
Wyndmere ND 58081

## FCC Amateur Radio Licenses in York

KB8OXD

Nathanael R Budd
4951 64th St NE
York ND 58386

N0IKJ
Ruth A Budd
4951 64th St NE
York ND 58386

W0TF
Richard M Budd
4951 64th St NE
York ND 58386

## FCC Amateur Radio Licenses in Ypsilanti

KC0KRR
Ron B Cruff Jr
114 2nd St S
Ypsilanti ND 58497

## FCC Amateur Radio Licenses in Zahl

W0YYN
Clifford C Christianson Sr
Zahl ND 58856

## FCC Amateur Radio Licenses in Zap

WB0NZJ
Harvey G Boehler
Zap ND 585800036